Other Titles in the Series

Abandonment to Divine Providence by Jean Pierre de Caussade

Imitating Christ in the Everyday: A Retreat with Thomas à Kempis

Athanasius' Life of St. Antony of the Desert: Monastic Manners for Today's World

The Soul of the Apostolate by Jean-Baptiste Chautard

Trustful Surrender: A Retreat Based on the Classic Writings of Fr. Jean Baptiste Saint-Jure, S.J., and St. Claude la Colombiere, S.J.

Advent and Christmas with the Church Fathers

Living True Ignatian Spirituality with St. Ignatius's Spiritual Exercises

Lent and Easter with the Church Fathers

The Image of God and Your Truest Self: A Retreat Based on the Classic Writings of the Church Fathers

Finding Your Virtues and Naming Your Vices: A Retreat Based on the Classic Writings of St. Thomas Aquinas

Setting the World on Fire: A Retreat with St. Catherine of Siena

Praying in and through the Dark Night with St. John of the Cross

PENTECOST

WITH THE CHURCH FATHERS

PENTECOST

WITH THE CHURCH FATHERS

A Seven-Week Retreat on the
Person and the Presence of the Holy Spirit

TAN Books
Gastonia, North Carolina

Cover design by Jordan Avery

ISBN: 978-1-5051-3151-2
Kindle ISBN: 978-1-5051-3152-9
ePUB ISBN: 978-1-5051-3153-6

Published in the United States by
TAN Books
PO Box 269
Gastonia, NC 28053
www.TANBooks.com

Printed in India.

"It is impossible to worship the Son except in the Holy Spirit; it is impossible to call upon the Father except in the Spirit of adoption."

—St. Basil of Caesarea, *On the Holy Spirit,* sec. 11.27

Come, Holy Spirit, fill the hearts of Your faithful and kindle in them the fire of Your love.
Send forth Your Spirit and they shall be created. And You shall renew the face of the earth.
O God, who by the light of the Holy Spirit did instruct the hearts of the faithful, grant that by the same Holy Spirit, we may be truly wise and ever enjoy His consolations.
Through the same Christ Our Lord. Amen.

Contents

Introduction

How to Approach These Pages

The Christian celebration of Pentecost commemorates the descent of the Holy Spirit upon Mary and the first disciples. Pentecost is to the Holy Spirit what Epiphany is to the Son: having been born from the pierced side of Christ on the cross, the Holy Spirit now manifests Christ's Church as the universal instrument of salvation, evidenced by visitors from all over the world coming to witness this new inbreaking of God's Spirit. Christ's nascent body is now empowered, inspired even, to go out into the world and proclaim that the Kingdom of God has now come for all.

That is why, fifty days after Easter, the Church receives the fullness of the Third Person of the Trinity. These fifty days would have naturally reminded the first Christians of their old Jewish feast of Weeks, during which they thanked Yahweh for His bounty, seven weeks after the first harvest of grain (see Ex 34:22). But now, instead of material sustenance, God sends His very self and shows how He longs to dwell personally in the souls of His chosen people.

Despite the haste with which this glorious event occurred, a theology and a spirituality of the Holy Spirit would take centuries to unfold. Unlike the Father and the Son, the Spirit, by His very name, is ethereal and abstract, not at all easy to imagine or define. But we can only love what we know, so greater love demands greater and greater knowledge and familiarity of one's beloved. Consequently, the Church spent the first few centuries defining and defending the divinity and the work of the Holy Spirit because the earliest theologians also knew that the more we could know accurately about God, the more ardently we would be able to love Him. Furthermore, in knowing and loving Him more deeply, we could more easily and readily discern what He desires to do in our lives.

This latest work from TAN Books, *Pentecost with the Church Fathers,* is a unique way to be with these early Christian thinkers as they came to reflect on the Person of the Spirit of God. Who is the Holy Spirit, and what are the effects of His indwelling in my life? How do the Sacred Scriptures portray Him, and how did the Church come to profess Him in her creeds and councils? Yet this book is not designed simply as a study in history but as a do-it-at-home retreat, a personal invitation to grow in mystical union with the Holy Spirit.

The following pages are divided into seven thematic chapters following the seven weeks between Eastertide and the Monday after Pentecost, the memorial of the Blessed Virgin Mary, Mother of the Church. Each week offers a focused collection of quotes from the Church Fathers along with salient selections from the Bible, the Holy Mass, or the *Catechism of the Catholic Church* regarding the Third Person of the Trinity. Each week also ends with the Gospel proclaimed that week at Mass.

Your task in working your way through each week is to meditate slowly on whatever passage or word or image resonates within you. Read and meditate while always asking what the Spirit might be trying to teach you at any given moment. *Multum non multa,* "much of one thing and not many things," is a classic Latin adage to keep in mind. If you find yourself drawn to a particular passage or word, stay there and ask the Holy Spirit why this struck you so strongly. As you ponder these words, you might be drawn to jot down what has resonated in your soul. To this end, along with each selection of text, you will also find space to answer some questions and jot down some thoughts. Spend time looking at these questions and (knowing of course that you can do with these whatever you wish) asking the Holy Spirit to direct you toward the exercises that might produce the greatest fruit.

This ancient practice of reflecting on one's own life presupposes that God is working in your life in a way that He is not working in anyone else's life. You are His beloved, and His message to you conforms perfectly to your own personal state in life, your occupation, family situation, and all the other experiences that make up the unique story which is your life. Being as concrete as possible is the Christian's way of fighting against the convenient temptation of keeping God solely in the spiritual, reducing Him to an abstract being whose presence is necessary only in times of trial or, as in the minds of most today, only at the time of death where it's your last chance to get it right. No, God is speaking to you now; He is speaking to you precisely as you are right now. What follows is TAN Books' invitation to sit prayerfully with some of the most foundational Christian thinkers, to read their words, and then for you to invite the Holy Spirit to descend freshly into each moment in your life as you concretely show Him that you are now ready to grow in holiness.

The ultimate question to contemplate as you begin this retreat is: Do I have a deep familiarity with the Third Person of the Holy Trinity, the Holy Spirit? In other words: Do I know who He is and what He does? Is the Holy Spirit real to me? Am I able to have a special friendship with Him, clearly different from my connection with God the Father and God the Son, Jesus Christ? Is the Holy Spirit someone whom I invite into my life, someone whose voice is familiar to me and whose promptings throughout the day I am able to recognize and trust?

When a Christian explicitly sets time aside for daily prayer or an annual retreat, it is an ancient practice to begin each morning of your day by immediately turning your thoughts to the theme or the word or the special virtue the Lord might be speaking to you about that very day. As we begin this retreat, think about getting a journal—a pad of paper or simple notebook would do—and using this to jot down the messages and feelings that will no doubt come through the indwelling of the Holy Spirit. As in any relationship between persons, the more intentional and generous you are with the other (even God), the more He can be with you. Like anything, deepening our prayer life requires the execution of a definite plan, so do not be afraid to tell God what it is you want each day and exactly what gifts you hope to receive from Him.

While we can rest assured God will in fact do what He promises, we, too, must put into practice what we are now setting out to do. So let's begin with some concrete particulars.

To begin, think about how true this is: You can only pray as you can, not as you can't. This axiom requires you to be honest with your own limitations and time commitments. You are (probably) not a monk or cloistered religious; you are (probably) a married person, maybe an extremely busy parent, someone living in the world of demands and deadlines, someone living out your God-given vocation in the messiness of the twenty-first century. That means you cannot pray as a desert hermit or a nun behind a grille; in fact, it would actually be sinful for you to try to find God outside the vocation He has given you. You are therefore to be "shrewd as serpents" (Mt 10:16) in figuring out how to let the Lord increase your holiness.

It is essential to remember that we cannot always control what comes in and out of our minds, but we can control our bodies. If you and the Lord determine that ten minutes, fifteen minutes, or a half hour (whatever it be) is what you will commit yourself to, stay there for that ten minutes, that fifteen minutes, or that half hour. Even if you are drifting off to sleep, even if your mind is racing elsewhere, be still. Be still and gently ask the Lord to help bring your consciousness back to His presence within and before you. What you do not want to do is to think, "Oh well, nothing is happening; I'll come back later." Let's face it. You probably won't come back later, because the kids will be home, you'll have to make supper, you'll be too tired, and so on. Commit yourself to a time and maybe even to a place and simply stay there. *That is your first and most fundamental commitment.*

Therefore, start by asking yourself and the Holy Spirit: How much time can I realistically devote to prayer each day? Be very truthful here: we rarely find the time; we must be intentional in carving out and making that time happen. What time of day is best for me to select that amount of time? Second: Where would I most in truth be able to do this—my bedroom, someplace in the house, in the car, at the office? In the end, begin with what is doable for you. Third: What do I truly want from this retreat? Where are my desires, my doubts, my fears, and my hopes? What do I want the Lord to know about me? What petition(s) do I want Him to hear and hopefully answer?

Ask the Holy Spirit to help you to answer and to commit to the following:

When you look ahead at the next seven weeks, how much time per day can you commit to meditating on these pages and giving yourself to private prayer?

I commit myself to ___________minutes of prayer each day, usually from _______to ________, and, when possible, at this place:_________________________.

Can you name what has motivated you to make this particular retreat at this time in your life?

Can you name the ways God might be speaking to you right now?

Where do you see the Holy Spirit at work? Do you talk to God in general or do you have a different relationship with God the

Father, God the Son, and God the Holy Spirit? How do you imagine each and interact with each differently?

We shall all, of course, have our own ideas swirling around these fundamental questions. We all have varied experiences of God's presence, and we are all unique and irreducible to anyone else. Your prayer life may look a lot like other Christians', but none of us will be identical in our desires and certainly not in our life's experiences. Nonetheless, God has each of us in mind as His beloved children and longs—yearns, even to the point of becoming one of us—to be more active in our lives. For this reason, the Holy Spirit has been sent not only "cosmically" but *personally* and *uniquely* into each of our lives. Our response must now be one of trust, trust that God loves us and thirsts for a deeper intimacy with us, and a desire on our part to know the Spirit and hear His voice.

Each of our seven weeks of retreat will begin with the theme for the Sunday Mass of that week. Between Easter and Pentecost, the Church works her way through the Acts of the Apostles and the Gospel of John. Every day's readings can be found on many websites (www.usccb.org, for example), and we encourage you to unite our retreat with the daily Mass readings. While the following is in no way a commentary on the Scriptures, all Christians must keep the Bible at the front and center of their prayer lives. This is the Word of God, the Word that points us to the Word, Jesus Christ. That is why Scripture and Sacred Tradition, as the two fonts of revelation, were given to us by Christ Himself. Keeping these two fonts together is your life as a Christian. It is for you that all of this was done, for your salvation and eternal joy. Consequently, be bold in bringing your daily experiences and fears and hopes and stresses to your prayer life and to the words that follow.

Week 1

The Holy Spirit in the Bible

Each daily liturgy through Easter week naturally focuses our attention on the risen Christ and how His first disciples came to receive the Good News of love's triumph over sin and death. Since the lectionary from which the Mass readings are proclaimed is divided into a three-year cycle, you may hear a Gospel on this Easter Sunday from:

> John 20:1–9,
> Matthew 28:1–10,
> Mark 16:1–7, or
> Luke 24:13–35.

As subtly different as each Gospel author portrays this pivotal scene, the message is the same: Jesus Christ is God Himself, and He alone can defeat all that we have freely put between ourselves and the Father.

Easter is not over today or even this week. Easter is completed only by Pentecost: there may be forty days of Lenten observance, but there are fifty days of Easter celebration. Easter is completed only by Pentecost because the work of Christ finds fulfillment in the work of the Holy Spirit. In fact, the Lord Himself tells us, "But I tell you the truth, it is better for you that I go. For if I do not go, the Advocate will not come to you. But if I go, I will send him to you" (Jn 16:7). As we shall see in the week to come, the Holy Spirit is already clearly active before Christ's coming to earth—He is present at creation symbolized by the "mighty wind," and He rushes upon Old Testament figures like Samson and King David. Yet it is the Sacred Triduum that unlocks the Holy Spirit's presence into the Christian people in a new and everlasting manner. It is the crucified heart of Christ that melts our hearts to the degree where we finally let another in, where we finally admit our need for a humble Savior. In this receiving of the wounded Christ, then, our hearts are prepared to become sharers in the Spirt who makes us children of the same Father as Jesus:

> After Christ had completed his mission on earth, it still remained necessary that we should become partakers and sharers of the divine nature of the Word. We had to give up our own life and be so transformed that we would begin to live an entirely new kind of life that would be pleasing to God. However, this was something we could do only by sharing the Holy Spirit. And the most fitting and appropriate time for the mission and descent of the Holy Spirit to us was . . . the occasion of our Savior's departure to heaven. As long as Christ was with them in the flesh, the believers would have thought that they possessed all the blessings he had to offer. But when the time came for him to ascend to his Father in heaven, it was necessary for him to be united through his Spirit to those who worshiped him and to dwell in our hearts through faith. Only by the Spirit's presence within us in this way could he give us the confidence to cry out, "Abba, Father," and enable us to grow in holiness.[1]

The possible Gospels for Easter Mass, whether it be the vigil or later Sunday morning Masses, the Gospel for years A, B, or C all focus our attention on the empty tomb. It is this tomb that ultimately saves our soul, yet the cross is what brings us face to face with what

---

1 Cyril of Alexandria, *Commentary on John*, 10.16.7, in *A Library of Father of the Holy Catholic Church Anterior to the Division of the East and West*, vol. 48 (Oxford: John Henry Parker Publishers, 1800-81), 443–44.

we have done and what we too would be if it were not for the grace of Jesus Christ. We are all sinners, and all have, therefore, merited death. But God loves us too much to let that happen, so as Adam and Eve were shamefully leaving Eden, God began to prepare the entire world for His Son's and Spirit's coming. Through the Old Testament figures, He foreshadowed the True Lamb of Sacrifice and manifested some of His Spirit's power to His chosen people.

The ascension of Jesus begins the great novena, the nine days between Christ's bodily return to the Father and the subsequent descent of the Holy Spirit. This great movement means great mystery, and we shall slowly unpack the implications of the Son's sending of the Holy Spirit as our retreat unfolds.

To begin, then, let us return to the source of God's Word to all of humanity, searching His Scriptures for the Holy Spirit's appearance and activity, focusing on His descent as portrayed by the Apostle Luke at the beginning of the Acts of the Apostles:

> When the time for Pentecost was fulfilled, they were all in one place together. And suddenly there came from the sky a noise like a strong driving wind, and it filled the entire house in which they were. Then there appeared to them tongues as of fire, which parted and came to rest on each one of them. And they were all filled with the holy Spirit and began to speak in different tongues, as the Spirit enabled them to proclaim. Now there were devout Jews from every nation under heaven staying in Jerusalem. At this sound, they gathered in a large crowd, but they were confused because each one heard them speaking in his own language. (Acts 2:1–6)

The word *spirit* can be used in diverse ways. We talk about the spirit of the age or the spirit of a room, team spirit, or even those flask-filling spirits that can inebriate. We talk about some people being in-spired, and today the word *spiritual* has oftentimes come to mean someone who might take the deeper things of life more seriously than most. Spirit can obviously mean many different things to many different people, a word that is difficult to restrict to any one particular definition.

Given this level of etherealness, why do you think the Third Person of the Trinity wants to be known initially as Spirit, describing Himself in Scripture as someone who is as agile as the wind but as important and divine as God?

Since we were little, we have probably imagined God the Father as an older gentleman sporting a big white beard; we all have had pictures of the Son as Jesus Christ who is depicted as a baby in Mary's arms and as a grown man who walked on dusty plains performing miracles and teaching crowds. We all have depictions of Jesus's crucifixion and can readily imagine His glory after His resurrection from the dead three days later. While these images tell us something certainly true, they are obviously our own depictions over the centuries. As insufficient as these pictures and portraits really are, however, we have an even less accurate image of the Holy Spirit. Even the Bible stretches to find symbols to describe Him: light as a breeze, zealous as fire, peaceful as a dove—very lithe and even lofty images, symbols that leave a lot more room for our own imaginations and definitions.

What do you know about the Holy Spirit? Can you list three images or words to describe Him in your life?

Describe a time you have felt close to the Spirit's presence.

Does the Spirit's invisible presence frighten you or comfort you? Why?

But who does the Bible say this Spirit is? Or more precisely, as the author of the Bible, who does the Holy Spirit Himself say He is? First, we should notice how He chooses to reveal Himself slowly, knowing our limited capacity to understand Him. Second, collaborating with the hands and the minds of each particular human author, the Holy Spirit prompted these men with the scriptural images, words, and wisdom that would become the fundamental basis of all Christian truth. Consequently, it is the Holy Spirit who covertly introduces Himself in the opening line of all Sacred Scripture: "In the beginning, when God created the heavens and the earth and the earth was without form or shape, with darkness over the abyss and a mighty wind sweeping over the waters . . ." (Gn 1:1–2).

The great Christian Tradition has always encountered all three of the divine persons of the Trinity in these words of the Spirit: "God" is the Father who creates; the "beginning" is the Son in whom the Father creates, providing the pattern and the promise of all creation (the word for "beginning" here is not the word for a temporal or chronological start but is the word for a "principle" or even an "archetype," the Son in whom all things have come to be; cf. Jn 1:3). Finally, that "mighty wind sweeping over the waters" refers to the Holy Spirit who informs all of creation by His universal presence.

> And the Spirit of God was borne upon the face of the waters. Does this spirit mean the diffusion of air? The sacred writer wishes to enumerate to you the elements of the world, to tell you that God created the heavens, the earth, water, and air and that the last was now diffused and in motion; or rather, that which is truer and confirmed by the authority of the ancients, by the Spirit of God, he means the Holy Spirit. It is, as has been remarked, the special name, the name above all others that Scripture delights to give to the Holy Spirit, and always by the spirit of God the Holy Spirit is meant, the Spirit which completes the divine and blessed Trinity. You will find it better therefore to take it in this sense. How then did the Spirit of God move upon the waters? It cherished the nature of the waters as one sees a bird cover the eggs with her body and impart to them vital force from her own warmth. Such is, as nearly as

> possible, the meaning of these words—the Spirit was borne: let us understand, that is, prepared the nature of water to produce living beings: a sufficient proof for those who ask if the Holy Spirit took an active part in the creation of the world.[2]

Saint Basil (d. 379), the very influential bishop of Caesarea in modern-day Turkey, makes sure his readers understand the Spirit's activity here "in this sense," realizing that the Spirit can be understood in various ways. The "special name" Basil knows Scripture uses for the Holy Spirit is the Hebrew *rûah*, and it is used almost four hundred times in the Old Testament.

God's chosen people saw in this term *rûah* three different uses. The first and most foundational usage is spirit as the "breath" of God that vivifies creatures. We see this right in the beginning when God breathes His own life into humanity, giving us our unique status as God's own images and likenesses: "Then the LORD God formed the man out of the dust of the ground and blew into his nostrils the breath of life, and the man became a living being" (Gn 2:7). A living thing breathes while one void of life does not, and the Jewish people understood that God had imparted His own divine life into all peoples, making all people images and likenesses of their heavenly Father.

The second use of *spirit* appears when selected individuals needed to be made more godlike in order to accomplish some task for the people of Israel. For instance, when Samuel anoints Saul as a prophet, He promises him that the power of God will be with him as he continues his journey as Israel's leader: "After that you will come to Gibeath-elohim, where the Philistine garrison is located. As you enter that city, you will meet a band of prophets coming down from the

---

2 St. Basil the Great, *Hexameron*, sec. 6; New Advent translation, https://www.newadvent.org/fathers/32012.htm. The New Advent website makes public the multi-volume Ante-Nicene Fathers, the Nicene Fathers, and Post-Nicene Fathers which arose out of the Oxford Movement. These volumes were English translations of the Fathers prepared by many scholars, British mainly (including St. John Henry Cardinal Newman), between 1886 and 1900. Philip Schaff was the first editor and he later asked Henry Wace to assist in this work when the second—and more expanded—series was commissioned.

high place. They will be preceded by lyres, tambourines, flutes, and harps, and will be in prophetic ecstasy. The spirit of the Lord will rush upon you, and you will join them in their prophetic ecstasy and will become a changed man. When these signs have come to pass, do whatever lies to hand, because God is with you" (1 Sm 10:5–7).

Christians read the Old Testament as the foreshadowing of all the perfect works God will do in Jesus Christ (that is what makes it "Old"). Here we can hear a faint glimpse of Mary's words to the wine stewards at Cana, "Do whatever he tells you" (Jn 2:5). For when the Spirit of God draws near, we are changed in that we now know we walk with God and have the confidence to overcome any trial or tribulation. As is the case with Saul here, the Spirit changes us, makes us more like God, enabling us to do supernatural things in accord with His own designs.

Second, this is how the Spirit is also depicted in the Old Testament as the one responsible for ordering creation and delivering the Father's bounty to those who hunger and thirst. The Spirit nourishes and protects. He redirects the sinner and even longs to renew all of creation to the Father's greater glory. Or as the Psalmist puts it: "All of these look to you to give them food in due time. When you give it to them, they gather; when you open your hand, they are well filled. When you hide your face, they panic. Take away their breath, they perish and return to the dust. Send forth your spirit, they are created and you renew the face of the earth" (Ps 104:27–30).

In the Old Testament, the Spirit is the principle of our existence, the One who constantly renews creation and directs the affairs of God's people. He thus empowers God's warriors (see Nm 27:18), judges (see Jdgs 13:25), and prophets, like Ezekiel: "I will give you a new heart, and a new spirit I will put within you. I will remove the heart of stone from your flesh and give you a heart of flesh. I will put my spirit within you so that you walk in my statutes, observe my ordinances, and keep them" (Ez 36:26–27). The Spirit of God was understood by the Jewish people to be a living extension of their one, true God, a moving and vivifying presence who gathered God's chosen ones into a fortified and flourishing people.

> Who gave you the ability to contemplate the beauty of the skies, the course of the sun, the round moon, the millions of stars, the harmony and rhythm that issue from the world as from a lyre, the return of the seasons, the alternation of the months, the demarcation of day and night, the fruits of the earth, the vastness of the air, the ceaseless motion of the waves, the sound of the wind? Who gave you the rain, the soil to cultivate, food to eat, arts, houses, laws, a republic, cultivated manners, friendship with your fellows?[3]

When was the last time you prayed outside? Have you taken the time lately to gaze upon the miraculous structure of some natural object, say, a tree or flower? Has nature's politicization by the "Green Movement" sapped your wonder in nature?

Are you able to gaze at the stars at night? Pay attention to all the various colors and smells and sights that surround us. All of these are God's first gifts to us, the beauty of His creation.

List three times, places or experiences you hold dear in your memory as times that God has spoken to you most powerfully of His Spirit's love for you:

1.________________________

2.________________________

3.________________________

---

3 Gregory of Nazianzus, *On Love for the Poor*, 23, in Olivier Clément, *Roots of Christian Mysticism* (Hyde Park, NY: New City Press, 1995), 17.

The third use of *spirit* is more reminiscent of what Christians imagine when they think of Pentecost. While the Holy Spirit is not yet totally understood as a separate and distinct divine person in the Old Testament (lacking any theology of the Trinity), the Jewish people do set the stage to understand God's Spirit as the uncreated expression of God's care. For instance, as God was forming His people, He begins to work on the malicious Pharaoh through Joseph, "a man so endowed with the spirit of God" (Gn 41:38). The same Spirit came upon Samson as he needed to achieve some superhuman feat: "But the spirit of the Lord rushed upon Samson, and he tore the lion apart barehanded, as one tears a young goat. Without telling his father or mother what he had done" (Jgs 14:6). Or, more notably, David was anointed king with the Spirit who promised never to leave him: "Then Samuel, with the horn of oil in hand, anointed him in the midst of his brothers, and from that day on, the spirit of the Lord rushed upon David" (1 Sm 16:13). Only through the Holy Spirit could a man come to repent and compose Psalm 51 after committing adultery and murdering the rightful husband of his concubine.

Even in the Old Testament, then, the Spirit of God imparts not only a natural life into us but a supernatural life as well. The Spirit enables us to speak the truth when difficult, to live each day when we feel like giving up, to overcome barriers and to live with purpose, integrity, and joy. Yet the Church Fathers could not equate the Old Testament figures' encounters with the Holy Spirit with the power of Pentecost. While the prophets and patriarchs, judges and kings of Israel were no doubt inspired by God, a new level of divine union was inaugurated by the life, death, and resurrection of Jesus Christ. The Spirit does not happen upon the scene only after Christ's ascension, for He has been at work since the foundation of the world:

> Therefore it is one and the same Spirit who is in the prophets, and in the apostles. He was, however, in the former only for awhile; whereas he abides in the latter forever. In other words, he is in the prophets but not to remain always in them; in the apostles, that he might abide in them forever. He has been

> apportioned to the former in moderation; to the latter, he has been wholly poured out; he was sparingly given to the one, upon the other lavishly bestowed. He was not however, manifested before the Lord's Resurrection but conferred by Christ's Resurrection. In fact, Christ said, "I will ask the Father, and he will give you another Advocate that he may be with you forever, the Spirit of truth" (Jn 14:16–17). . . . Since the Lord was about to go to heaven, he had to give the Paraclete to his disciples, that he might not leave them orphans (cf. Jn 14:18), as it were, and abandon them without a defender or some sort of guardian. That would not have been proper at all.[4]

When you try to picture yourself in the presence of the Holy Spirit, what images or feelings surface?

What areas in your life do you need the Holy Spirit to reveal Himself right now?

Have you ever read the Old Testament? Is this something to which the Spirit might be calling you to study?

---

[4] Novatian, *On the Holy Spirit*, 29, in *Novatian: The Trinity*, trans. Russell DeSimone (Washington, DC: Catholic University of America Press, 1972), 100–1.

This imparting of the Spirit's supernatural life becomes all the clearer when we "fast forward" many centuries up to the first Pentecost. Here in first century Jerusalem, the Holy Spirit brings us all back to the very first moment of creation. The Holy Spirit again descends and watches vigilantly over what God has now formed. This time, however, it is not simply creation in general but His newly-formed apostolic and Marian Church, a people singularly known and called out of the world to be living icons of God on earth.

> All these devoted themselves with one accord to prayer, together with some women, and Mary the mother of Jesus, and his brothers. . . .
>
> When the time for Pentecost was fulfilled, they were all in one place together. And suddenly there came from the sky a noise like a strong driving wind, and it filled the entire house in which they were. Then there appeared to them tongues as of fire, which parted and came to rest on each one of them. And they were all filled with the Holy Spirit and began to speak in different tongues, as the Spirit enabled them to proclaim. (Acts 1:14; 2:1–4)

With her head now fully ascended into heaven, the Body of Christ—the visible Church—can now receive the Holy Spirit in a new and definitive way. Now the Holy Spirit opens up God's nature to us even more, revealing our God as a Trinity available to all persons in any part of the globe, uniting them in one common language of Love: "Go, therefore, and make disciples of all nations, baptizing them in the name of the Father, and of the Son, and of the holy Spirit" (Mt 28:19).

We who live in this post-Pentecostal life of the Church sometimes forget that God has revealed His personal essence as a Trinity of Love carefully and slowly. When first asked who He was, God simply told Moses, "I am who am" (Ex 3:14). This name provided centuries of philosophical reflection, seeing in it the one unique being whose very nature it is to exist. As the chosen people journeyed through the centuries, however, God began to show His truest nature to us gently, so as not to disturb a strict Monotheism while granting glimpses into His triune life. "The Lord sent the Paraclete because, since human weakness could not receive everything at once, it might gradually be directed and regulated and brought to perfection of discipline by the Lord's vicar, the Holy Spirit."[5] Ever mindful of our littleness, God gently reveals the fullness of his triune life in a time and in a manner He knows allows us the greatest opportunity to understand it properly.

The Church Fathers thus argued that God revealed the Trinity in accord with our capacity to receive such a truth:

> The Old Testament has manifested the Father clearly, the Son only dimly. The New Testament has revealed the Son and implied the divinity of the Holy Spirit. But today the Holy Spirit lives among us and makes himself more clearly known. It would actually have been dangerous to proclaim openly the Son while the divinity of the Father was not fully acknowledged, and then, before the divinity of the Son was accepted, to add as it were the extra burden of the Holy Spirit's divinity. . . . So it was more fitting that by adding a little at a time and, as David says, by ascending from glory to glory, the splendor of the Trinity should shine forth progressively.[6]

In so doing, Jesus began to teach about the Holy Spirit in whom He was anointed and whom He would pledge to His disciples: "If you love me, you will keep my commandments. And I will ask the Father, and he will give you another Advocate to be with you always, the Spirit of truth" (Jn 14:15–17). With this introduction, Jesus has finally felt confident that His followers would understand that He has never acted alone: they know He has come from the Father and now He wants them to know He is sending "another Advocate."

---

[5] Tertullian, *On the Veiling of Virgins*, 1, in *Ancient Christian Commentary on Scripture: New Testament IVb on John 11-21*, trans. Oden (Downers Grove, IL: InterVarsity Press, 2007), 206.

[6] Gregory of Nazianzus, *Fifth Theological Oration*, sec. 31.26, in *Roots of Christian Mysticism*, 61.

But now I am going to the one who sent me, and not one of you asks me, "Where are you going?" But because I told you this, grief has filled your hearts. But I tell you the truth, it is better for you that I go. For if I do not go, the Advocate will not come to you. But if I go, I will send him to you. And when he comes he will convict the world in regard to sin and righteousness and condemnation: sin, because they do not believe in me; righteousness, because I am going to the Father and you will no longer see me; condemnation, because the ruler of this world has been condemned. I have much more to tell you, but you cannot bear it now. But when he comes, the Spirit of truth, he will guide you to all truth. He will not speak on his own, but he will speak what he hears, and will declare to you the things that are coming. He will glorify me, because he will take from what is mine and declare it to you. Everything that the Father has is mine; for this reason I told you that he will take from what is mine and declare it to you. (Jn 16:5–15)

Have you ever thought about God's revealing truths carefully and only in accord with our ability to understand? Could you see this same dynamic in your own life, that God's not showing you something until you were ready to receive it?

Does it comfort you to know that your Advocate before the Father is the Holy Spirit, the Spirit of Love? He sees every pulse of your heart, every secret smile and joy, every desire you have ever had. Does this truth of who you truly are before God console or frighten you?

The word *Advocate* is often translated as "Comforter" or "Paraclete" as well. "When he proclaims and promises the coming of the Holy Spirit, Jesus calls him the 'Paraclete,' literally, 'he who is called to one's side,' *ad-vocatus*. 'Paraclete' is commonly translated by 'consoler,' and Jesus is the first consoler. The Lord also called the Holy Spirit 'the Spirit of truth'" (CCC 692).

The words translated as "Comforter" or "Consoler," whether from the Latin *Advocatus* or the Greek Paraclete, were originally found in ancient legal terminology and refer to a trusted confidant who would stand by your side and intercede for you before a tribunal. This witness was someone whom you could trust with all that was involved in your particular case and someone who would appeal to the judge on your behalf in the most charitable and forgiving manner possible.

The root of both these terms for the Holy Spirit (*vocare* in Latin, *kalein* in Greek) has the sense "to call," reminding us that God calls each of us by name (see Is 43:1). The Spirit of God knows us better than we know ourselves, loves us more than we love ourselves, and He longs to put right all the messiness of our busy lives. Or as St. Augustine famously wrote, God is even closer to us than we are to ourselves—"more intimately present to me than my innermost being, and higher than the highest peak of my spirit."[7] This is the call we have received through the Holy Spirit's indwelling: to know that we have been brought into an intimate relationship with God, so intimate we have now become, through grace, what Jesus Christ is by nature—a child of the Father.

> When I think of the profusion of the names of the Spirit, I am seized with dread: Spirit of God, Spirit of Christ, Spirit of Adoption, and on and on. He renews us in baptism and resurrection. He blows where he wills. Source of light and life, he makes of me a temple, he makes me divine. . . . Everything God does is done by the Spirit. He multiplies himself in tongues of fire and he multiplies his gifts by raising up preachers, apostles,

---

7 Augustine, *Confessions*, 3.6.11, trans. Maria Boulding (Hyde Park, NY: New City Press, 1997), 83.

prophets, pastors, teachers. . . . He is another Comforter . . . as if he were another God.[8]

Does the Spirit's knowledge of your entire self bring you comfort or unease? Why?

Do you feel prompted to tell God anything about yourself at this moment? What is it?

"For those who are led by the Spirit of God are children of God. For you did not receive a spirit of slavery to fall back into fear, but you received a spirit of adoption, through which we cry, 'Abba, Father!' The Spirit itself bears witness with our spirit that we are children of God, and if children, then heirs, heirs of God and joint heirs with Christ, if only we suffer with him so that we may also be glorified with him" (Rom 8:14–17).

That is why Jesus teaches us how to pray beginning by calling upon our common Father in heaven. "He was praying in a certain place, and when he had finished, one of his disciples said to him, 'Lord, teach us to pray just as John taught his disciples.' He said to them, 'When you pray, say: Father, hallowed be your name, your kingdom come'" (Lk 11:1–2). In this brief snapshot of Jesus's own prayer life, there are four points worth mentioning.

The first is that Jesus, the eternally begotten Son of God, *prays*. Jesus prays. So, if the One who is forever one with the Father and who is forever in heaven prays, how much more should we? We are

8 Gregory of Nazianzus, *Fifth Theological Oration*, sec. 29, in *Roots of Christian Mysticism*, 73.

funny amphibians, made for heaven but caught up in life on earth. We need to make the time and the effort to uncover each day our true vocation as saints.

Second, that is why we can ask to learn to pray. "If you then, who are wicked, know how to give good gifts to your children, how much more will the Father in heaven give the Holy Spirit to those who ask him?" (Lk 11:13). That is exactly what you are doing in this at-home retreat. We can ask the Holy Spirit to show us the best ways we can commune with the Father—with our morning coffee or not, inside or outside, with some music or only silence, and so on.

Third, notice Jesus goes to "a certain place." That is what we discussed at the beginning of our retreat: be intentional, pick a time and a place where prayer can really "happen" for you. Be specific and purposeful that the time you and the Spirit have decided on is both optimal and practical.

And the final lesson leads us to a much larger point: calling upon our Father's name as something made holy or "hallowed." Jesus Christ is the one naturally-born Son, but we are the Father's adopted sons and daughters—two different ways of being a child of God, but both children all the same. And how does our brother Jesus tell us to begin? By acknowledging the holiness of the Father's name: *Our Father, hallowed be your name!* Have you ever thought of a name as holy? We shall discuss this later in the fifth week, but here lies an ancient insight: Having access to one's name shows a particular intimacy or grasp of who that person is. To know another's name is to have a certain "in" with them, maybe even a certain type of power over them. To share your truest name with another is an invitation toward trust and the possibility of an ongoing relationship.

As a definite person of the Most Holy Trinity, the Spirit is to be called upon as such, a distinct and nameable individual. As persons, the Father and the Son and the Holy Spirit ask to be known as each is. That is why there is an entire commandment teaching us about the holiness of a name. When we are in an intimate relationship with another, we not only know his or her name but might even have a special name used only between us. There are of course levels of intimacy measured by a name we use for another: addressing someone as Mr. or Mrs. is different from calling them Joseph or Mary, and a much different level when that person could be Hon or Sweetie, a special name reserved for a very intimate few.

Each time you pray the Our Father, then, think why you call God's name *holy* or *hallowed*. God has granted you access to His very being, allowing you to call upon Him. That admittance is not something we should ever use flippantly or rely on simply to release anger or frustration. "You shall not invoke the name of the LORD, your God, in vain. For the LORD will not leave unpunished anyone who invokes his name in vain" (Ex 20:7). Preaching on the Sermon on the Mount, Saint Augustine put it this way:

> This petition is not made as if God's name were not hallowed but so that people may hallow it, that is, so that God may be so well known to them that they would not consider anything else more hallowed which they would more dare to offend. . . . And so his name is said to be holy whenever it is spoken of with reverence and with fear of giving offence. This is what is now happening when, by making it known throughout the different nations, the Gospel proclaims the name of the one God through the mediation of his Son.[9]

Knowing God has revealed His name to us as something holy changes us, not Him. It changes us because, finally in our lives, there is something holy, absolute, and beyond utility or flippancy. It is an encounter that is to be revered and adored, and thus life-changing. In realizing deeply that God is your *Abba* is to bring about a new life for you, now as a son or daughter of a heavenly Father:

> "Pray thus," Jesus says: "Our Father who are in the heavens." Anybody who is renewed, reborn, and restored to his God by grace, first of all says, "Father," because he is now become a son or daughter. It is said: "He came to his own, and his own did not receive him. To as many as did receive him he gave them power

9 Augustine, *Sermon on the Mount*, 2.5.19, in *The New Testament I&II*, trans. Michael Campbell (Hyde Park, NY: New City Press, 2014), 78.

> to become the children of God, who believe his name" (Jn 1:11). Whoever therefore believes in his name is made a child of God, and hence should begin to give thanks and show himself a child of God as the names his Father as God in heaven. He bears witness also, among the first of his words at his rebirth, that he renounces his earthly and fleshy father and acknowledge that he has begun to have the Father in heaven as his only Father.[10]

While the Old Testament warns against using God's name in a offhand or glib manner, Jesus, in the New Testament, invites us to call God Father. Even our earthly fathers are not wholly "father," as they are first a son. By extension, of course, the name of the Son and the Holy Spirit are equally as holy, to be invoked only when calling out to God in loving faith. These are not names to be bandied about when frustrated or released only when angry as so many do. "You shall not invoke the name of the LORD, your God, in vain" (Dt 5:11; see also CCC 2142). The Church Fathers linked the first two commandments, making God the only one worthy of our adoration and His name not to be used in vain, something we spurt out when irritated. For if God were truly my only God and Lord, I would not "use" Him only when I was in need of release or, even worse, feeling like cursing a situation or another person.

What in your life do you consider "holy," that about which you are never flippant or dismissive?

How does genuflecting and kneeling before the Blessed Sacrament make you feel? Do you see this as the one place of absolute worship in your life?

---

10 Cyprian of Carthage, *On the Lord's Prayer* 9, in *Tertullian, Cyprian, Origen On the Lord's Prayer*, trans. Alistair Stewart-Sykes (Crestwood, NY: St. Vladimir's Press, 2004), 70–71; slightly adjusted.

You may not think of yourself as having idols, but where do you place most of your trust or spend most of your energy when worried? Is it your finances, your social status, your physical health, your technology? Can you place all of these very real and important concerns in your Father's will, in His Son's pierced hands?

In the Church's unbroken theology, the presence of the Holy Spirit elevates us into the status of God's children. We are no longer servants who obey God out of fear of punishment; we are no longer soldiers who do what is asked only for the sake of reward. No, we are now sons and daughters, sharing the same Spirit as God Himself: "As proof that you are children, God sent the Spirit of his Son into our hearts, crying out, 'Abba, Father!' So you are no longer a slave but a child, and if a child then also an heir, through God" (Gal 4:6–7).

> We would be overwhelmed in our awareness of being slaves, we would disintegrate in our earthly condition, if the authority of the Father himself and the Spirit of his Son were not rousing us to make this acclamation. "God sent," it says, "the Spirit of his Son into our hearts crying out, 'Abba, Father!'" Our minds grow faint, our flesh falters at divine matters, if God who gives the command were not to carry out himself what he commands to be done. When have mortals dared to call God their Father except now, when the deepest recesses of the human being are enlivened by power from heaven?[11]

Have you ever been totally honest with yourself and asked, "Why do I call myself a Christian?" Is it because of your fear of hell (slave) or reward of heaven (soldier)? Is it because you

[11] St. Peter Chrysologus, *Sermon* 71,3, in *St. Peter Chrysologus: Selected Sermons*, trans. William Palardy (Washington, DC: Catholic University of America Press, 2004), 286.

simply want to be one with the Lord (son or daughter) and thus love and be loved by Him, no matter what He asks of you?

> Seeing that there is such an order and unity in the Holy Trinity, who could separate either the Son from the Father, or the Spirit from the Son or from the Father himself? Who could be so audacious as to say that the Trinity is unlike itself and different in nature? Or that the Son is foreign to the Father in substance? Or that the Spirit is estranged from the Son? . . . First, let him divide the Radiance from the Light or the Wisdom from the Wise One, or else tell us how these things are possible. But if this cannot be done, much more is it the audacity of the insane to ask such questions about God. For the divinity is not handed down through logical demonstrations and arguments, as has been said, but by faith and by pious reasoning joined with reverence.[12]

As we witness here, fourth century rhetoric was powerful and to the punch. Who would be so "insane" and so bold as to tell the Holy Spirit that He and the Father and the Son were not one? This is audacious, to separate the only three Divine Persons; in fact, Saint Athanasius warns it's not even possible! Do you know what is audacious? When we call God our Father: "At the Savior's command, and formed by divine teaching we dare (*audemus dicere*) to say . . ."

---

12 Athanasius, *First Letter to Serapion* 1.20.1-3, in *Works on the Spirit: Athanasius and Didymus*, trans. Mark DelCogliano et al (Yonkers, NY: St. Vladimir's Seminary Press, 2011), 84.

Pray the *Our Father* slowly and see if any one word or phrase resonates deeply within you.

How does it feel to know and call upon God as "Father"? Do any important images from your own earthly father come to mind?

At this point in our retreat, you might feel excited. You may be wondering if anything is "happening," or if you are doing enough. Be assured: Simply desiring to give this time to God is the beginning of greater holiness. We may not always be consistent, and we rarely do great feats of love, but we can long for God, and in His gracious mercy, maybe that is all He is asking of you right now. "The entire life of a good Christian is a holy desire. What you desire, however, you don't yet see. But by desiring you are made large enough, so that, when there comes what you should see, you may be filled."[13] Of course, growing in union with the Holy Spirit will prove to be more than a holy desire, but we are just beginning. For now, rest assured that the Lord delights in you and that you are on the right track.

Whom do you love most tenderly? Name them.

Are your actions consistent with your holy desires for those you love?

---

13 Augustine of Hippo, *Homilies on First John* 4.6, in *Homilies on the First Epistle of John*, trans. Boniface Ramsey (Hyde Park, NY: New City Press, 2008), 69.

How do you interact with that person, those persons, on a daily basis? Do you ever take them for granted or take your frustrations out on those you have in mind?

Do you see your love for these persons not as a projection of your own emotions but as a real manifestation of the Holy Spirit in our lives? If so, do you love with the Spirit's virtue and selflessness in mind or do you still love based on your own feelings and emotions?

Do you ever divide your loves into ones that are "natural" and ones that are "holy"? If so, try to reunite those people into one love, into one God-given desire for greater union and charity toward all those people God has put into your life.

The Spirit testifies to the Father's love and longing to dwell even more intimately in our lives. "Man, however, by the power of the Spirit and the spiritual regeneration, not only comes to the measures of the first Adam, but is made greater than he. Man is deified. . . . As the Lord put on the body, leaving behind all principality and power, so Christians put on the Holy Ghost, and are at rest."[14] As the Son of God who was once spirit only put on flesh in the womb of Mary, we who are embodied since conception are invited to put on the Spirit at baptism. He is the "rest" that our restless hearts seek, the way into the Trinity for whom we have been created.

Part of a retreat is to examine the past year in one's life and ask: Where you have found God and where have I felt restless? Take some time to jot down the most memorable blessings of this past year as well as to list some place where stress and anxiety have been unfortunately overwhelming.

---

14 Macarius of Egypt, *Spiritual Homily* no. 26.2 and .15, in *Fifty Spiritual Homilies of Macarius the Egyptian*, trans. A. J. Mason (New York: MacMillan Company, 1921), 185, 192.

Week 2

The Holy Spirit in the Creed

One of the most beloved popes, Saint John Paul II (1978–2005), decreed the Second Sunday of Easter as Divine Mercy Sunday. As one who was forced to grow up literally between barbarous Nazis to the west and atheistic Communists to the east, someone who personally pardoned his own assassin, John Paul knew the meaning of mercy. Drawing from his Polish heritage that celebrated the spirituality of Saint Faustina Kowalska, OLM (1905–38), John Paul enshrined the heart of her visions and interlocutions with Jesus by establishing the Church's feast of Divine Mercy.

For all three liturgical years—A, B, and C—the Gospel for this week is:

> John 20:19–31.

Here we are brought into the upper room with our attention focused on two central moments. The first is when Jesus institutes the sacrament of Reconciliation by breathing the Holy Spirit upon the Apostles who are thereafter enabled to forgive sins. This is the divine mercy available to us each day of the week right down the street in the local parish's confessional. As we prepare for Pentecost, we see in this act the Lord's imparting of the Holy Spirit on His apostolic Church, empowering these, the first bishops of the Church, to act in His name to absolve sinners. "[Jesus] said to them again, 'Peace be with you. As the Father has sent me, so I send you.' And when he had said this, he breathed on them and said to them, 'Receive the Holy Spirit. Whose sins you forgive are forgiven them, and whose sins you retain are retained'" (Jn 20:21–23).

The second moment fixes our eyes on doubting Thomas, who insists on placing his hands into the wounds of the crucified Christ. What is striking about this encounter is that, as Jesus showed His followers His wounds, they rejoiced. Usually, wounds bring about reactions of fear or anger, even revenge. But in Jesus Christ, our wounds, our sins, and our hiddenness can be occasions of rejoicing. "When he had said this, he showed them his hands and his side. The disciples rejoiced when they saw the Lord" (Jn 20:20). Here, Thomas comes to see that sinners are loved not despite their moral failings but precisely because of them: the wounds and those places of emptiness and regret are precisely where Jesus's grace can fill up in us what is lacking. Through these torments, He can finally enter and be received as Savior and merciful Redeemer.

This week, pay special attention to all the varied ways the resurrected Christ appears to His disciples. We read how He appeared to them in the open, spoke to them plainly, ate with them, and, in the words of Pope Leo the Great:

> allowed himself to be touched with a loving and earnest touch by those who were being grazed by doubt. He went through a closed door to the disciples. By his breath he gave them the Holy Spirit. When they had been given the light of understanding, he opened up to them the hidden things of the Holy Scriptures. He showed them the wounds in his side, the places of the nails, and all the signs of his recent suffering, so that the property of the divine and of the human natures might be understood as remaining inseparable in him.[1]

Pope Leo provides for us a perfect model of Catholic theology and spirituality. He ponders the scene in Scripture, and then, under

1 Leo the Great, sermon 71.3, in *St. Leo the Great: Sermons*, trans. Jane Freeland (Washington, DC: Catholic University of America Press, 1996), 313.

the guidance of the Holy Spirit, he seeks to show all the mechanics behind the event. Here, for instance, he uses the wounds of Christ to show His humanity and His imparting of the Holy Spirit to prove His divinity yet again.

We must understand that the Bible was not written *to* us but *for* us. This is God's word for us today, but this word is not a dead letter on a page; it is a living invitation in and through the people of God, Christ's Body on earth. That is why the most accurate readers of the Bible approach the Scriptures through the ongoing, divinely-safeguarded two-thousand-year tradition of the Church.

> Having, as we have said, received this message and this faith the church, though dispersed over all the world, guards them as carefully as though it lived in one house, believes them as with one soul and the same heart, and preaches, teaches and transmits them in unison, as with one mouth. For even if the languages of the world are different, the meaning of the tradition is one and the same. The churches founded in Germany have not believed differently or transmitted the tradition differently—or the ones founded among the Iberians, the Celts, in the east, in Libya, or in the center of the earth.[2]

For example, all Christians must believe in the Trinity, in the dual-nature of Christ's divinity and humanity, in the absolute sanction against abortion and infanticide, and so on. But where are those absolutes laid out in Scripture?

These truths are certainly hinted at, and arguments are obviously made that they are scriptural, but if they were undeniably clear, Christian bodies would not split up over their particular interpretation of Scripture. Even what books belong in the Bible are not listed in the Bible; obviously the Bible depends on the Sacred Tradition of the Christian community. In fact, just such a community, based upon and led by the Apostles, preceded any written word

---

[2] Ephiphanius of Salamis, *Panarion* 31:1 (dated around 375), in *The Panarion of Epiphanius of Salamis, Book I, Sects 1-46*, trans. Frank Williams (Leiden: Brill Publishers, 2009), 203.

by decades. "'Therefore, brethren, stand fast and hold the traditions which you have been taught, whether by word or by our letter' (2 Tim 2:15). From this it is clear that they did not hand down everything by letter, but there was much also that was not written. Like that which was written, the unwritten too is worthy of belief. So let us regard the tradition of the Church also as worthy of belief. Is it a tradition? Seek no further."[3]

> I believe that you once heard this from me, but I, nonetheless, repeat it now as well. My mother, who followed me to Milan, discovered that the Milanese church did not fast on Saturday; she began to be upset and to be in doubt about what to do. At that time I was not concerned about such things, but on her account I consulted Ambrose, a man of blessed memory, on this point. He replied that he could teach me nothing but what he himself did, since, if he knew a better rule, he would follow it instead. I had thought that he meant to advise us not to fast on Saturday without giving any reason, but by his own authority alone; yet he went on and said to me, "When I go to Rome, I fast on Saturday; when I am here, I do not fast. So to whatever church you go, observe its custom if you do not want to be a scandal to anyone or anyone to be a scandal to you." When I reported this rule to my mother, she willingly made it her own. But I thought of this statement again and again, and I always regarded it as if I had received it from a heavenly oracle. For I often saw with sorrow and grief that many of the weak are upset by the quarrelsome stubbornness or superstitious timidity of certain brothers. For they stir up such quarrelsome questions in matters of this sort that cannot be brought to a definite end by the authority of holy scripture or by the tradition of the universal Church or by the benefit of amending one's life.[4]

---

3 John Chrysostom, *Homilies on the Second Epistle to the Thessalonians*, 4.2, in *The Faith of the Early Fathers*, vol. 2, trans. W. A. Jurgens (Collegeville, MN: The Liturgical Press, 1979), 124 (no. 1213).

4 Augustine, *epistle* 54.3, in *Letters 1-99*, trans. Roland Teske (Hyde Park: New City Press, 2001), 211. Note that this advice from Bishop Ambrose is the

The two main sources of revelation since the beginning of Christianity are indisputably holy Scripture and the Tradition of the universal Church, and Augustine even acknowledges that what one does for "the benefit of amending one's life" is also a reliable (but hardly inerrant) way we might also see how God leads His people.

More to our point, where does the Bible tell us that the Holy Spirit is God pure and simple, coeternal and equally glorious with the Father and the Son? It does not. But not to worry, for even the Bible tells us that we need another font of noncontradictory revelation to ensure what we have received through the scriptural authors is understood correctly. This is the meaning of tradition, literally "to hand over," and that is why the Church Fathers not only looked at the letters of Holy Writ but also developed the conciliar tradition of speaking through the right way to understand the Bible: "Therefore, brothers, stand firm and hold fast to the traditions that you were taught, either by an oral statement or by a letter of ours" (2 Thes 2:15).

To this end, there is a very insightful story in Saint Luke's Acts of the Apostles when he describes the scene of an Ethiopian eunuch who, while traveling to Jerusalem to worship God, reads the Prophet Isaiah. As he is caught up by the prophecy of the Suffering Servant and wondering what this all meant, "The Spirit said to Philip, 'Go and join up with that chariot'" (Acts 8:29). Philip then asks the eunuch if he actually understood what he was reading. This curious court official rightly responds, "How can I, unless someone instructs me?" (Acts 8:31). With that, the apostle Philip explains how to understand the pages of the Bible, what they really mean, and how the passage he was reading (Is 53:7–8) was all about Jesus Christ, the one true Lamb.

---

source of the better-known rendition, "When in Rome, do as the Romans do."

As we move from focusing on the Bible to how the Bible is most accurately read and lived out, do you appreciate the need for the apostolic Tradition to interpret the Bible correctly?

If the Bible was all we needed for holiness, why are there thousands of *sola scriptura* Christian communities in the United States alone? Take time to thank God for sending His Holy Spirit to guide the Church, His Church, and for safeguarding her, the Bride, against all serious error, thereby keeping her "without spot or wrinkle" (Eph 5:27), despite the sins of all her members.

As we saw in week 1 when we traced the Holy Spirit's presence throughout the unfolding of Sacred Scripture, God in His infinite wisdom slowly revealed Himself as three distinct Persons. In the beginning, God first wanted to make sure we understood that He is one and there is no other. In fact, Jesus tells us that belief in one God only, monotheism, is the first and most foundational tenet of belief: "Jesus replied, 'The first is this: Hear, O Israel! The Lord our God is Lord alone!'" (Mk 12:29). This is the monotheism that was unique to the Jewish people.

But once God decreed that the "fullness of time" (Gal 4:4) had come, only then did He begin to reveal Himself as a Father with an eternally beloved Son whom He sent to earth as Jesus Christ. Since Christianity grew out of Judaism, the monotheism of the Jewish people had to be opened up cautiously and gently. While the Jewish people knew God the Father, and while they did indeed anticipate the coming of their Messiah, they did not yet have the understanding that this Chosen One would be a divine person, equally God, of the same substance as the Father. That is why Jesus Christ only slowly showed Himself to be this beloved and begotten Son of God so as to win over as many monotheists as possible.

This explicit identity with God the Father is precisely what would cost Jesus His life: "'The Father and I are one.' The Jews again picked up rocks to stone him. Jesus answered them, 'I have shown you many good works from my Father. For which of these are you trying to stone me?' The Jews answered him, 'We are not stoning you for a good work but for blasphemy. You, a man, are making yourself God'" (Jn 10:30–33).

Yet, at other times, Jesus seems to make Himself somehow less than God. "Jesus answered him, 'Why do you call me good? No one is good but God alone'" (Lk 18:19); or again, "The Father is greater than I" (Jn 14:28). As the Church expanded, a greater understanding of the relationships between Father, Son, and Holy Spirit was thus needed. Greater depth would not only provide more insights for the faithful but also give the Church the needed terminology and theology to defend herself against accusations of polytheism. To ensure such needed truths, Jesus promised that He would send "another Advocate" (Jn 14:16), and this same Spirit guides the Church's theology even today.

The theological battles in the early Church were really all about reading the Bible correctly. Some read it carefully, always in line with the established traditions of liturgy, prayer, and conduct as found throughout the Church, while others tend to veer off from those canonical norms into areas of novel interpretations and eventual heresy. This is why theology and spirituality interpenetrate each other in the life of a Christian: we meet God in both our brains as well as in our hearts. Yet, in the time of the Church Fathers, it seems that theological issues mattered much more to the Christian faithful than dogma does today.

In fact, Gregory of Nyssa (d. 395) tells an enjoyable story that might be a bit of a stretch, but it certainly captured much of the tone of a fourth-century Constantinopolitan marketplace where pagans shopped alongside Catholics, and where even those Christians could not yet agree on how best to explain the persons of the Trinity:

> The entire town teems with disputation: the plazas, the markets, the crossroads and alleys are all full of it. Men who trade in cloth, those who change our currency, the food vendors and all the others spend their days arguing. If you ask one of them for change, he philosophizes about what it means to be "Begotten" and "Unbegotten." If you ask, "How much is a loaf of bread?", the response you get is that "The Father is greater than the Son." When you ask if your bath is ready, the steward answers that, "The Son must be made out of nothing."[5]

Such a tale may seem fanciful today, but that is the point. It shouldn't be! Our older brothers and sisters in the Catholic Faith took their theology seriously, and so should we. It was really the Enlightenment of the seventeenth and eighteenth centuries that popularized the separation of religious "experience" from the importance of dogma. As a consequence, religion was reduced to simply fulfilling one's Sunday duties and explained as a matter of feeling and emotion; doctrine became something superfluous, necessary only for the doctors of theology comfortably cloistered in their ivory towers.

But this is to do the Christian faith a great disservice. Love and knowledge are inseparable, and that is why we must pledge ourselves to contemplating our Bible intelligently, commit ourselves to a daily rhythm of prayer that bears fruit, and avail ourselves of regular confession and daily reception of Jesus in Holy Communion when possible. But in all of this, we must foster the habit of speaking to the Lord from our hearts, from the stresses and commitments of our everyday lives. Speaking "heart to heart" is how we move from being mechanically "sacramentalized" in the Faith to being mystically evangelized, allowing ourselves to be ignited by the

---

5 Gregory of Nyssa, *On the Deity of the Son and the Holy Spirit, Patrologia Graeca* 46, 557B, our translation.

Son in the Spirit and thereby become responsible and reliable stewards of the graces God the Father puts into our souls.

But how do we explain one God in these three Persons? The Bible surely hints at it, but nowhere is a definition easily forthcoming, nor anywhere do we find enough theological depth to defend the common heresies of the first Christians. The two most common Trinitarian heresies tried to protect the unity and transcendence of God while still trying to regard the Son and the Spirit as divine, but not as divine as God the Father. On the one hand, there was a priest in Rome named Sabellius (d. c. 230) who established what we came to call modalism: namely, God is one (so far, so good) and He simply appears in three different modes—at one time Father, at another Son, and later as the Holy Spirit. These three are not distinct Persons but three temporary and interchangeable manifestations of the one God, the way the same pail of water can appear as ice or steam.

On the other hand, the Alexandrian priest Arius kept the one true God safely above any division by subordinating the Spirit to the Son and the Son to the Father. In this way, he avoided accusations of polytheism and instead pictured the Father having two "lesser" deities in His Son and Spirit, thus safeguarding His own unique status as God.

To read the Bible correctly, and in order to combat modalists and Arians who sapped the Trinity of any real communion (for true unity requires both an equality as well as differentiation in persons), other theologians drew from the best of Greek philosophy to explain God as a single unity of substance but a diversity of Persons. A faint analogy might be the way we talk about humanity in the singular but simultaneously understand there to be a plurality of Persons sharing in that one nature or substance.

The very influential theologian, catechist, and astute reader of Scripture Origen (d. c. 254) read in the Gospel of John a clear teaching of the three divine Persons in the one divine nature:

> There is this distinction of the three persons in the Father and the Son and the Holy Spirit, which is recalled in the plural

> number of the wells. Yet of these wells there is one spring. For the substance and nature of the Trinity is one. But John has carefully expressed the mystical language, so that what was said in the plural of the persons would be in keeping with the substance in the singular. But he has carefully expressed the mystical language, so that what was said in the plural of the persons would be in keeping with the substance in the singular.[6]

According to Origen, then, John mystically introduced the seeds of a Trinitarian theology by distinguishing the one spring or source of Godliness, the one divine substance, from the three wells which would be revealed carefully. Such a distinction is exactly what the early Church had to do: to show how the biblical seeds of the Trinity were true and logical when fully understood.

A major advancement in this needed clarification was the start of the ecumenical council, an assembly of the bishops of the Church and their leading theologians. This desire for harmony was not limited to Church officials. Instead, because unity was so important to the success of the emperors of Rome, once Christianity proved on the ascendancy, it was in the emperor's best interest to ensure that the Christian people were not divided over essential questions of doctrine. The first emperor to be baptized was Constantine (d. 337). In order to guarantee that Christians under his rule professed Jesus Christ as one with the Father ("consubstantial" as we say today), he renewed an ancient tradition started by the Apostles (as evidenced in Acts 15 and the Council of Jerusalem) when the Apostles gathered to discuss the proper approach for reaching out to the Gentiles.

That is, in 325, Constantine ordered all the Catholic bishops from around the known Christian world to gather in Nicaea (not far from his palace) in modern-day Turkey to address the divine status of the Son. The second ecumenical council was called in 381 by an even more faithful and doctrinally sound emperor, Theodosius I (d. 395), who needed the bishops to declare the Holy Spirit

---

6 Origen, *Homilies on Numbers* 11, in *Origen: Homilies on Numbers, Ancient Christian Texts,* trans. Thomas P. Scheck (Downers Grove, IL: Intervarsity Press, 2009), 63.

also one in being with the Father and the Son. Clearly, while no ancient culture had a problem imagining their God as some sort of Father or Overseer, to introduce the Son and the Holy Spirit as equally divine and equally worthy of worship demanded some work, and to work the early Church went, trusting that it was the Holy Spirit who safeguarded the unassailable truths of the Church when it came to faith and morals.

> The Church's preaching is everywhere established and continues the same, and has testimony from the prophets and apostles, and all the disciples throughout the beginnings and the middle times and the end, yes, throughout God's whole economy and the secure working that tends toward salvation and is operative in our faith. This faith we safeguard, having received it from the Church. It is like some excellent deposit in a suitable vessel, that always under God's Spirit, rejuvenates itself and rejuvenates the vessel in which it is.
>
> For this, God's gift, has been entrusted to the Church, as the life-breath to the first-fashioned, so that all the members receiving it might be vivified. And in this gift has been deposited the Communion of Christ, that is, the Holy Spirit, the pledge of imperishability, the strength of our faith, and the ladder of ascent to God. . . . Of him (i.e. the Spirit) all those do not partake who do not agree with the Church, but defrauded themselves of life by their evil doctrines and wicked practices. For where the Church is, there is the Spirit of God, and where God's Spirit is, there is the Church, and all grace: and Spirit is Truth.[7]

Do you appreciate what a gift you possess in having been brought into this Church, the very Body Christ Himself founded? When did that happen?

[7] Irenaeus of Lyons, *Against the Heresies* 3.24.1, in *St. Irenaeus of Lyons: Against the Heresies* in *Ancient Christian Writers*, trans. Dominic J. Unger (Mahwah, NJ: The Newman Press, 2012), 110.

Who has best exemplified a truly Catholic way of life for you?

Do you pray to the Holy Spirit that He be able to reunite all Christians once again around the same altar?

Do you pray for those in the world who do not yet know Jesus Christ as their Lord and Savior?

With Christians severely divided over how to speak about and possibly adore the Son and the Spirit, Emperor Constantine grew worried about factions growing within his empire. Christians were growing in both number and influence, and their cohesion only bolstered Constantine's need for imperial unity. To achieve such harmony, Emperor Constantine called for the Church's first ecumenical council in 325. By divine decree, he ordered all bishops convene in Nicaea, a small place in modern-day Turkey, very near his royal palace and accessible for the clergy from both the east and the west.

This gathering was really aimed at the heretic Arius, whom we met earlier. Remember, according to Arius, the Son of God was indeed the Savior of the world but He could not be co-equal to the Father; that is, He could not be unqualifiedly "God" without compromising God's unity. If the Father was God and if Jesus was also equally God, would that not mean there were at least two Gods? This was how Arius explained his way out of this conundrum: that "before he was begotten or created or appointed or established, the Son did not exist . . . for the Son has a beginning, but God is without a beginning." In one way, Arius's sentiments were correct: certainly one of the characteristics of God is that He does not have a beginning or is somehow brought into being by another.

Therefore, the bishops allowed Arius and his followers to state their views and the debate started. The agreed upon result was the Nicene Creed, which established how Christians were to profess their faith at Mass and in their own prayers, in part teaching:

> We believe in one God, the Father almighty,
> maker of all things visible and invisible;
> And in one Lord, Jesus Christ, the Only Begotten Son of God,
> Eternally begotten from the Father,
> God from God, light from light,
> true God from true God, begotten not made,
> consubstantial with the Father,
> through Whom all things came into being,
> things in heaven and things on earth,
> Who because of us men and because of our salvation came down,
> and became incarnate and became man, and suffered,
> and rose again on the third day, and ascended to the heavens,
> and will come to judge the living and dead,
> And in the Holy Spirit.
> But as for those who say, "There was a time when
> he [the Son] was not,"
> and, "Before being born He was not,"
> and that, "He came into existence out of nothing,"
> or who assert that, "the Son of God is of a
> different hypostasis or substance,"
> or is "created," or "is subject to alteration or change"
> —these the Catholic and apostolic Church anathematizes.

Notice what was at stake here in 325: the consubstantial nature of the Son and the Father, the fact that they share the same divine substance or nature. The Son is in fact begotten but eternally so: there was never a time when the Father was not a Father and, therefore, never a time when the Son was not. This relationship between Father and Son is eternal, for what it means to be Father is to have a Son, and what it means to be Son is to have a Father.

Notice in the history of the Church the Holy Spirit's existence is not yet in need of explanation. Belief in the Holy Spirit's existence is simply stated. Nothing more. Instead, the original Nicene Creed ends with a series of anathemas or condemnations. These ultimatums were directed at Arius and his disciples, those who wanted to subordinate the Son to the Father, making the Son a lesser deity who had not always existed and was therefore of a different nature.

Emerging from this Council of Nicaea was a young theologian, the future bishop of Alexandria, Athanasius (d. 373). His writings would help the Church explain both the consubstantiality of the Father and the Son, as well as their distinct personal relationship to each other. They are different not *in what they are as God* but *in who they are as Father and as Son*. In other words, the Father and the Son and the Holy Spirit in no way differ in their substance as "divine" or as "God"—the same way you and I do not differ in degree in our being human—but the Father, Son, and Spirit do differ in who they are as distinct from one another. How so? By means of their relationship to one another: in that the Father is Unbegotten, the Son is Begotten, and the Spirit is He who proceeds from this eternal union.

> And it was God's will, that the Summary of our Faith should have the same bearing. For he has bid us be baptized, not in the name of Unoriginate and Originate, not into the name of Uncreate and Creature, but into the name of Father, Son, and Holy Spirit, for with such an initiation we too are made sons and daughters verily, and using the name of the Father, we acknowledge from that name the Word in the Father. But if he wills that we should call his own Father our Father, we must not on that account measure ourselves with the Son according to nature, for it is because of the Son that the Father is so called by us; for since the Word bore our body and came to be in us, therefore by reason of the Word in us, is God called our Father. For the Spirit of the Word in us names through us his own Father as ours, which is the Apostle's meaning when

he says, "God has sent forth the Spirit of His Son into your hearts, crying, Abba, Father" (Gal 4:6).[8]

Mainly because of his constant conflict with Arius and his followers (many who were influential Romans), Athanasius received the nickname *Athanasius Contra Mundum*, "Athanasius Against the World." The fourth century would have looked a lot different if this man had not helped the Church formulate a rich theology of the Trinity. What Athanasius did was truly inspired: he both ensured the eternal equality of the Father and of the Son and of the Holy Spirit, while also emphasizing our ability to participate in that community of love, thereby transforming us into the children of that same Triune God.

At Mass, do you simply recite or do you pray the Creed? Please pray carefully over each line and let the Holy Spirit speak to you as He wills.

When you think about Jesus Christ, do you tend to think of Him more as human or more as divine? What factors might influence you here?

Can you appreciate the beauty of the Incarnation, that although just as equally God as the Father, the Son chose to become a human and thus learn to live and make friends and hold a job and honor His mother and father and all the other things we as men and women must learn to do?

---

8 Athanasius of Alexandria, *De Decretis* §31, New Advent translation, https://www.newadvent.org/fathers/2809.htm. slightly adjusted.

We who theologize after two thousand years of solid Catholic thought can take so much for granted. Despite the growing consensus and theological brilliance of the fourth century, matters of the Trinity and of the Holy Spirit in particular were far from settled. That is why by 381, another ecumenical council had to be called. This would be known as the First Council of Constantinople, called by the emperor Theodosius.

This became a needed opportunity to put any lingering Trinitarian heresies to rest. The council fathers therefore mentioned the third century error of Sabellius (a heresy teaching that the Father, Son, and Holy Spirit are simply three different names or "modes" of the one, relation-less divine substance), who so stressed the unity of God that any biblical references to "Father" and "Son" and "Spirit" were simply naming different manifestations of the one true God. As if the same water could be manifested as steam, liquid, or ice depending on the temperature, Sabellius thought of God as revealing Himself as Father at one point in time, as the Son in Jesus Christ at another, and eventually as the Holy Spirit. The council also took to task the Eunomians, extreme followers of Arius, who denied the Son was even somehow like the Father, instead stressing the utter difference between the two.

By the end of the fourth century, the Arian tendency to subordinate the Son to the Father was being widely applied to the divinity of the Holy Spirit. Even though by this time Arius and his closest friends had perished, a form of Arianism continued to linger—this time in the form of Pneumatomachianism, a fancy Greek word for "Those Who Combat the Spirit." The Pneumatomachi, led by Macedonius—a heretical bishop of Constantinople—denied the full divinity of the Holy Spirit. For these cynics, the Spirit was just a force, a power emitted from God but in no way God. In response, the Church gathered for the first time in Constantinople and reaffirmed all the teachings of Nicaea sixty years earlier and supplemented what she needed to in order to promote the divinity of the Spirit, thereby completing the Creed with the following:

> I believe in the Holy Spirit, the Lord, the giver of life, who proceeds from the Father, who with the Father and the Son is adored and glorified, who has spoken through the prophets.
>
> I believe in one, holy, Catholic and apostolic Church.
>
> I confess one Baptism for the forgiveness of sins and I look forward to the resurrection of the dead and the life of the world to come. Amen.

Sound familiar? In fact, the creed every orthodox Christian believer professes—Catholics on Sundays and on major celebrations—professes is technically the Nicene-Constantinopolitan Creed, begun in 325, nearly completed in 381, and finished, surprisingly, in 589, as we shall later see.

The Spirit here is professed to serve two functions. First, He is the giver of true life, a fitting image since any life demands "breath," which the Spirit is. Second, First Constantinople makes explicit that the Holy Spirit is also the one who spoke through the Old Testament prophets, preparing them to recognize the Messiah when at last He came. Relying on a rather lengthy passage from Saint Basil of Caesarea's *On the Holy Spirit*, we can see these two points as they are taking shape in the Church Fathers and thus in our Sacred Tradition:

> Let us return to the point we first raised: that in everything the Holy Spirit is indivisibly and inseparably joined to the Father and the Son. . . . If God is recognized to be present among the prophets because their prophesying is a gift of the Spirit, let our opponents determine what place they will give to the Holy Spirit. Will they rank him with God, or will they push him down to a creature's place? . . . Likewise the Son works as the Father's likeness, and needs no other cooperation, but he chooses to have his work completed through the Holy Spirit. "By the Word of the Lord the heavens were made, and all their host by the Spirit of his mouth" (Ps 32:6 LXX). The Word is not merely air set in motion by the organs of speech, nor is the Spirit of his mouth an exhalation of the lungs, but the Word is he who was with God in the beginning and was God and the

> Spirit of God's mouth is the Spirit of truth who proceeds from the Father. Perceive these three: the Lord who commands, the Word who creates, and the Spirit who strengthens.[9]

The "breath" represented by the Holy Spirit is not simply the bestowal of biological life but a life of truth, a life of virtue in Jesus Christ. The sacrament of Confirmation is clearly echoed here: "the Spirit who strengthens." Also clearly stated here is how the Spirit must be consubstantially divine if we regard God's chosen people divinely inspired at all (and no good Christian can disregard their older Jewish brothers and sisters). The Spirit of God had prepared the way for the Son's incarnation since the time of creation, inspiring patriarchs and prophets like Moses and Isaiah.

This is why immediately after the first Pentecost, Jesus's followers began to see that it was the Holy Spirit speaking the truth about the Christ throughout the Old Testament. Praying to God, they cry out, "You said by the Holy Spirit through the mouth of our father David, your servant: 'Why did the Gentiles rage / and the peoples entertain folly? / The kings of the earth took their stand / and the princes gathered together / against the Lord and against his anointed'" (Acts 4:24–26, quoting Ps 2:1–2). It was the Holy Spirit who inspired the patriarchs and prophets and the kings and judges of Israel to prepare the way of Christ by foreshadowing Him in all their words and ways. Since the foundation of the world, there was never a time when the Spirit of God was not at work. "Then beginning with Moses and all the prophets, he interpreted to them what referred to him in all the scriptures" (Lk 24:27).

Returning to the fuller exposition of the Holy Spirit as declared at I Constantinople, notice also how the Spirit *proceeds*, unlike the Son who is *born of the Father*. For if the Spirit were begotten, the Father would have two sons. Instead, the Spirit is spirated, the breath with which the Father speaks His Word *before all ages*. For the Father loves the Son so perfectly and so eternally that this love is actually a

---

9 Basil of Caesarea, *On the Holy Spirit* §16.38, trans. David Anderson (Crestwood, NY: St. Vladimir's Seminary Press, 1980), 60–63.

person, a divine Person, the Holy Spirit. There is no succession, no time or delay in this community of love: the Father speaks the Word in the Spirit, the Lover begets the Beloved in Love. "We neither say that the Holy Spirt is unbegotten—for we know one Unbegotten and one Beginning of beings, the Father of our Lord Jesus Christ—nor do we say that he is begotten: for in the Tradition of the Faith we have been taught that there is only one Only-Begotten. We have been taught that the Spirit of Truth proceeds from the Father, and we confess that he is uncreatedly from God."[10]

Saint Basil of Caeserea was the main leader and organizer of the three Cappadocian Fathers (so-called after the middle of modern-day Turkey, Cappadocia): Basil himself (d. 379), his brother Gregory of Nyssa (d. 395), and their dear monkish friend Gregory of Nazianzus (d. 390). The great contribution of these three men was their ability to keep the noxious tentacles of Arianism from creeping further and further. Just because a council declares a thought or thinker heretical does not mean that that is the end of the story (think of how many Catholics today are still fighting over the meaning of Vatican II). Subordinating the Son as well as the Spirit to the Father's unique status as the only God in and of Himself was an attractive position for much of the fourth century and even beyond.

The Cappadocian Fathers knew the Holy Spirit was sent into the world to unite humanity into a single body of praise, the Church. The Spirit would lead us into a new Eden, that place of harmony where our desires would be aligned with the good, stressing how the Holy Spirit can do for us what He first did for Mother Mary: incarnate the divine Son into each of our lives.

> The Spirit is described to be of God, not in the sense that all things are of God, but because he proceeds from the mouth of the Father, and is not begotten like the Son. Of course, the "mouth" of the Father is not a physical member, nor is the Spirit a dissipated exhalation, but "mouth" is used to the extent

---

10 St. Basil, *The Transcript of Faith*, in *Faith of the Early Fathers*, vol. 2, 5.

> that it is appropriate to God, and the Spirit is the essence of life and divine sanctification. Their intimacy is made clear. . . . He is also called the Spirit of Christ, since he is naturally related to him. That is why Scripture says, "Anyone who does not have the Spirit of Christ does not belong to him" (Rom 8:9). Only the Spirit can adequately glorify the Lord: "He will glorify me" (Jn 16:14), not as a creature, but as the Spirit of truth, since he himself is truth shining brightly.[11]

What does it mean for you to glorify the Lord?

List three ways you glorify the Lord at this point in your life:

1.____

2.____

3.____

Can you entrust the Spirit with these desires, asking Him to make them as real as He can in you at this point in time?

Of all the contributions the Cappadocian Fathers made to the Church's understanding of the Trinity, perhaps the most attractive was their understanding that what the Holy Spirit did for Jesus Christ He also longs to do for us. That is, the Spirit prepared a creature—namely, the Virgin Mary—to receive the divine Son, and by

---

11 Basil of Caesarea, *On the Holy Spirit* §46, p. 73.

extension, that same Spirit will prepare other creatures to receive Jesus in their souls.

Gregory of Nazianzus was the most reclusive and monastic of the three Cappadocians. In fact, he relinquished his call as bishop to retire to a more contemplative life, returning to his writing and poetry. The Arian factions must have been relieved, knowing in Gregory they had a formidable enemy who never doubted that the Spirit was one with the Father:

> The Holy Spirit, then, always existed, and exists, and always will exist. He neither had a beginning, nor will He have an end; but he was everlastingly ranged with and numbered with the Father and the Son. . . . Therefore he was ever being partaken, but not partaking; perfecting, not being perfected; sanctifying, not being sanctified; deifying, not being deified; himself ever the same with himself, and with those with whom he is in communion—invisible, eternal, incomprehensible, unchangeable, without quality, without quantity, without form, impalpable, self-moving, eternally moving, with free-will, self-powerful, All-powerful . . . Life and Lifegiver; Light and Lightgiver; absolute Good, and Spring of Goodness; the Right, the Princely Spirit; the Lord, the Sender, the Separator; Builder of his own Temple; leading, working as he wills; distributing his own Gifts; the Spirit of Adoption, of Truth, of Wisdom, of Understanding, of Knowledge, of Godliness, of Counsel, of Fear (which are ascribed to him) by whom the Father is known and the Son is glorified; and by whom alone he is known; one nature, one service, worship, power, perfection, sanctification.[12]

Under the influence of the Cappadocian Fathers, the Council of First Constantinople reaffirmed the consubstantiality of the Son while also explicitly affording the same and equal divine substance to the Holy Spirit. In fact, the tried-and-true phrase "one substance, three persons" is known as the Cappadocian Formula, as it best

---

12 Gregory of Nazianzus, *Oration* 41.9, New Advent translation, https://www.newadvent.org/fathers/310241.htm, slightly adjusted.

encapsulates the contributions of Basil, his brother Gregory of Nyssa, and their friend Gregory of Nazianzus.

The number of bishops at I Constantinople was around 180, approximately 150 who would sign on to the proceedings affirming the divinity of the Holy Spirit. The rest were labeled heretics due to their unwillingness to denounce their Arian tendencies and to assent to the true nature of the Son and the Spirit. These were duly deposed and exiled, while the orthodox Churchmen returned to their respective sees. A year later, the emperor Theodosius asked for local bishops to regather in the imperial city in order to reaffirm what the council laid out and to address more practical and logistical matters. At this Synod of Constantinople of 382, those gathered issued this decree:

> We have endured persecutions, afflictions, imperial threats and savagery from government administrators, as well as countless other trials by those heretical to the Faith. These we withstand for the sake of the true evangelical Faith explicated by 318 fathers who gathered in Nicaea in Bithynia. You, we, and all who are not bent on distorting the true Faith should therefore approvingly assent to this creed. For it holds the most ancient exposition of the Faith, wholly in accord with our baptism. This creed instructs us how to believe rightly in the name of the Father and of the Son and of the Holy Spirit. This creed has us assent firmly to the fact that the Father, the Son and the Holy Spirit are a single Godhead and power and substance. These three are one dignity deserving the same honor and co-eternal authority, but also exist in three wholly perfect hypostases, three perfect persons.
>
> As such, Sabellius' contaminated belief (i.e., Modalism) which confuses the persons and thus empties each of them from their own proper characteristics has absolutely no place here. Neither do the blasphemies of the Arians, the Eunomians (extreme Arians), and the Pneumatomachi have a place—for these heretics all break up the divine substance of the one Godhead. They thereby wrongly introduce some new nature (neither God nor creature) brought forth after God, a different

nature now introduced into the uncreated, consubstantial, and co-eternal Trinity.[13]

While the First Council of Constantinople and the work of the Cappadocians helped put to rest any Arian tendencies in the East, in the West, the tendency to subordinate the Son and the Spirit to the Father was still prevalent in particular areas, especially in the far western parts of the empire where the Greek-speaking councils had waned in their influence. To combat this, local synods were being held in today's Italy, France, and Spain. One of the threats to the Church's unity during this time was lower Europe's encounters with the Gothic cultures of the north, which still held on to various forms of Arianism.

In 589, almost one hundred bishops from the West met for the third time in Toledo, Spain, to discuss how to evangelize most effectively to those who still felt safer having only one divine Person, relegating the Son and the Spirit to an inferior place. On May 4, 589, the bishops met and fasted for days before convening for their deliberations. Focusing their thoughts mainly on John 15:26, "When the Advocate comes whom I will send you from the Father, the Spirit of truth that proceeds from the Father, he will testify to me," it was decided that the best way to show the divinity of the Son and of the Spirit was to stress how the Spirit comes directly from the Father *and from the Son*. In this way, the unity of the three divine Persons was upheld, reinforcing an image of a Godhead that "unfolds" a Trinity of Persons rather than a God who first has a Son and then a Spirit coming forth. This notion of divine unity was essential for upholding the Catholic Faith, so important that the bishops in Toledo added one—but very loaded—Latin word to the Nicene-Constantinopolitan Creed: *filioque*, a Latin phrase meaning "and the Son."

---

13 *A Letter of the Bishops Gathered in Synod in Constantinople* in 382 as found in Theodoret's Greek, *Church History* 5.9 (PG 82.1211-18) and in Cassiodorus' Latin *Three-Part Church History* 9.14 (*Patrologia Latina* 69.1130-33), our translation.

> I believe in the Holy Spirit, the Lord, the giver of life, who proceeds from the Father *and the Son*, who with the Father and the Son is adored and glorified, who has spoken through the prophets.

The western bishops as well as the pope saw this not so much as an addition but a completion of what the Church had always taught, the theory of double procession, that the Spirit proceeds as the Love between the Father *and the Son*.

As the centuries went on, the East and the West began to face competing cultures and differences in worship and liturgy. By the eleventh century, too many injuries and debates had unfortunately occurred, giving way to the Great Schism between the Catholic and the Orthodox Christians in 1054, making the *filioque* the flashpoint over which the schism supposedly occurred, though many other points of contention made any kind of rapprochement humanly impossible.

Today, the *Catechism of the Catholic Church* sees this history in this way:

> At the outset the Eastern tradition expresses the Father's character as first origin of the Spirit. By confessing the Spirit as he "who proceeds from the Father", it affirms that he *comes from* the Father *through* the Son. The Western tradition expresses first the consubstantial communion between Father and Son, by saying that the Spirit proceeds from the Father and the Son (*filioque*). It says this, "legitimately and with good reason", for the eternal order of the divine persons in their consubstantial communion implies that the Father, as "the principle without principle", is the first origin of the Spirit, but also that as Father of the only Son, he is, with the Son, the single principle from which the Holy Spirit proceeds. This legitimate complementarity, provided it does not become rigid, does not affect the identity of faith in the reality of the same mystery confessed. (CCC 248)

When you think of the Holy Spirt processing from the Father and the Son, do any images come to mind?

Do you pray for Catholic reunion between the East and the West? Do you pray for total reunion for these Catholic and Apostolic communities with our Protestant brothers and sisters?

What are some avenues of evangelization you can take with those you know?

Much of this later conciliar theology looked to arguably the most important Church Father in the history of Christianity, Saint Augustine of Hippo. In his massive *On the Trinity* (*De Trinitate*), Augustine teaches that the Spirit proceeds from both the Father as well as the Son, and that the divine unity demands such a unified origin: "We must confess that the Father and the Son are the origin of the Holy Spirit, not two origins, but just as Father and Son are one God, and with reference to creation one Creator and one Lord, so with reference to the Holy Spirit they are one Origin."[14] As Love Himself, it is fitting that the Holy Spirit proceed from both the Father and from the Son, as love is always the result of a lover and a beloved, as we shall later see.

As we leave the week of Divine Mercy Sunday, we do well to recall the etymology of that word *mercy*, coming from the Latin

---

14 Augustine, *On the Trinity* 5.15, trans. Edmund Hill (Hyde Park, NY: New City Press, 2012), 199.

misericordia. This term is made up of two beautiful words, *miser*, meaning "pity" or "pathetic," and *cor*, the Latin word for one's heart. This may seem like an ironic, if not unfortunate, combination of words, but the ancient meaning of being merciful is to be pitiable of heart, to be just sore enough so as to make room for another. Only the starving hunger, only the lonely desire communion, and, in our case, only the hurting can commiserate with those who desire mercy. The forgiven forgive, or at least they should: "His master summoned him and said to him, 'You wicked servant! I forgave you your entire debt because you begged me to. Should you not have had pity on your fellow servant, as I had pity on you?'" (Mt 18:32–33).

> We are to discuss, then, what being merciful or kindhearted essentially is. It is nothing other than feeling a soreness of heart caught from others. It gets its Latin name, *misericordia*, from the sorrow of someone who is miserable; it is made up of two words, *miser*, miserable, and *cor*, heart. It means being heartsore. So when someone else's misery or sorrow touches and pierces your heart, it's called *misericordia*, or soreness of heart. Our lives are really an expression of being merciful or heartsore. For example, you offer some bread to a hungry man; offer sympathetic kindness from the heart; don't do it contemptuously, or you'll be treating a fellow human being like a dog. So when you perform a work of mercy, if you're offering bread, feel sorry for the hungry; if you're offering drink, feel sorry for the thirsty; if you're handing out clothes, feel sorry for the naked; if you're offering hospitality, feel sorry for the stranger and traveler; if you're visiting the sick, feel sorry for the people who are ill; if you're burying the dead, feel sorry for the deceased; if you're patching up a quarrel, feel sorry for the quarrelers. We do none of these things, if we love God and our neighbor, without some sorrow of heart. They are good works which confirm that we are Christians.[15]

In the Christian Tradition, it is never enough simply to act on an external: our mercy will be measured not only on what we

---

15 Augustine, *Sermon* 358A (delivered possibly around 411) in *Sermons*, trans. Edmund Hill (Hyde Park, NY: New City Press, 1997), 196.

have doled out but, more importantly, the charity in our hearts for those whom we are serving. This Augustine calls a "sorrow of heart" because it moves us to see others as children of the same heavenly Father. Pride can sometimes make us look down on the needy, treating them "like a dog," but Christian mercy recognizes the inherent equality between all people, regardless of their current lot in life.

Now we can see how this week fits in perfectly with our Pentecost retreat: The Holy Spirit is the one who pours love into our hearts (see Rom 5:5), and He can find a place for charity only where there is emptiness, where there is a yearning for more. The poor of heart are the only ones who realize that they need a savior, and for this, God lowers Himself to our level. "For we do not have a high priest who is unable to sympathize with our weaknesses, but one who has similarly been tested in every way, yet without sin. So let us confidently approach the throne of grace to receive mercy and to find grace for timely help" (Heb 4:15–16). As we ponder the presence and the power of the Holy Spirit in our lives, let us pray for the grace to receive, not produce, this mercy and grace who is the Lord Jesus Christ. For holiness is not measured by great miracles but by the extent to which we allow Jesus and His Spirit to dwell in us. This is the grace of Baptism, where we turn next.

Week 3

The Holy Spirit at Baptism

In this week's Sunday Gospel, when Jesus appears to His disciples—whether it be on the road to Emmaus, back in the Upper Room, or on the waters of Tiberius, He shatters categories and reveals Himself in the everyday lives of His followers. These Gospels include:

> Luke 24:13–35,
> Luke 35–48, and
> John 21:1–19 or John 21:1–14.

No matter which of these you hear proclaimed this week, Jesus promises to meet you where and as you are. Take this seriously, for often we think we have to fix ourselves up before we are ready to meet Christ. The hard truth is that we simply cannot fix ourselves; rather, our only option is to let Jesus do the work. We are fallen and the only way "up" is through a mediator who is, first, able to heal us (Jesus as fully divine) as well as, second, able to be one with us and so transmit that divine remedy (Jesus as fully human).

Moreover, we must allow this encounter to occur as Jesus sees fit rather than the way we think it has to be. The devil tries to convince us that we can meet God only in "religious" events or buildings or only during acts of extreme piety. But if Jesus is the Lord of all and the Holy Spirit descends where He wills, a growth in holiness for each of us is to widen our categories regarding how and when and where the Lord can meet us.

> Do you not see that he does not remain with them continually, nor is his presence with them the same as before? He appeared, for instance, in the evening, and then disappeared. Then after eight days he appeared once again, and again he disappeared. Then he appeared later by the sea, and then another time, causing great awe. But what does John mean when he says Jesus "showed" himself? It is clear from this that he was not seen unless he condescended to be seen because his body was from this time forward incorruptible and of unmixed purity. But why has the writer mentioned the place? To show that Jesus had now taken away the greater part of their fear so that they now ventured out from their home and went about everywhere. For they were no longer shut up at home but had gone into Galilee to avoid dangers from the Jews. Simon, therefore, comes to fish. For since neither Christ was with them continually, nor was the Spirit yet given (i.e., at Pentecost), nor were they at that time yet entrusted with anything so had nothing to do, they returned to their trade.[1]

> We know that Peter was a fisherman, whereas Matthew was a tax collector. Peter returned to fishing after his conversion, but Matthew did not again sit down to his business of tax collecting, because it is one thing to seek to make a living by fishing and another to increase one's gains by money from the tax office. For there are some businesses that cannot—or hardly can—be carried on without sin. And these cannot be returned to after one's conversion.[2]

The early Church's emphasis of taking Luke 24 or John 21 as windows into how the Lord meets us in our everyday lives is a

---

1 John Chrysostom, *Homilies on the Gospel of John* 87.2, New Advent translation, https://www.newadvent.org/fathers/240187.htm.

2 Gregory the Great, *Forty Gospel Homilies*, 24, in *Ancient Christian Commentary on Scripture*, trans. Thomas Oden (Downers Grove, IL: InterVarsity Press, 2007), 379.

constant across the Eastern and Western fathers. But this sense of openness never overshadowed the one particular way Christ wants to begin His life with us in the sacrament of Baptism. This week we shall therefore prepare for Pentecost by looking at the mystical life started in those seemingly normal waters of the baptismal font. There is no other way to the Father than through Jesus Christ (cf. Jn 14:6), He who tells us the Apostles to go and baptize in the name of the Father, the Son, and the Holy Spirit (cf. Mt 28:18–20).

Where do you most easily sense the presence of God in your life?

Do you see your life as a vocation or have you divided it up into "career" and "vocation"? What might the difference be for you?

How might you widen your understanding of God to encounter Him more readily?

This encounter with Christ can be painful and it can be scary, but there is no other way. A wonderful scene in *The Chronicles of Narnia* between the Christ-figure Aslan the Lion and a girl named Jill helps us see what it means to surrender to Christ when and where He appears:

> "Are you not thirsty?" said the Lion.
>
> "I'm dying of thirst," said Jill.

"Then drink," said the Lion.

"May I—could I—would you mind going away while I do?" said Jill.

The Lion answered this only by a look and a very low growl. And as Jill gazed at its motionless bulk, she realized that she might as well have asked the whole mountain to move aside for her convenience. The delicious rippling noise of the stream was driving her nearly frantic.

"Will you promise not to—do anything to me, if I do come?" said Jill.

"I make no promise," said the Lion.

"Do you eat girls?" she said.

"I have swallowed up girls and boys, women and men, kings and emperors, cities and realms," said the Lion. It didn't say this as if it were boasting, nor as if it were sorry, nor as if it were angry. It just said it.

"I daren't come and drink," said Jill.

"Then you will die of thirst," said the Lion.

"Oh dear!" said Jill, coming another step nearer. "I suppose I must go and look for another stream then."

"There is no other stream," said the Lion.[3]

Christ refuses to let our indecision and fears drive Him away, and that is the theme of the Third Week of Easter. If you are making this at-home retreat, you are most likely baptized into a Christian community of one denomination or another. If you are not baptized, this week will be even more essential because we are going to study and pray about what one receives when baptized. In other words, what exactly happens to a baptized person?

As we have been making our way toward Pentecost, we have been tracing how the Holy Spirit was explained over the centuries, first in the sacred pages of the Bible and then in the sacred

---

[3] C. S. Lewis, *The Silver Chair* (New York: Harper, 1953), 21–23.

Tradition of Jesus's Church. We now telescope this theology into our souls in order to understand just what we were offered when we approached—or, very likely, were carried to—the baptismal font. "Then Jesus approached and said to them, 'All power in heaven and on earth has been given to me. Go, therefore, and make disciples of all nations, baptizing them in the name of the Father, and of the Son, and of the Holy Spirit, teaching them to observe all that I have commanded you. And behold, I am with you always, until the end of the age'" (Mt 28:18–20).

The Church Fathers took carefully the "order" of the divine Persons which Jesus taught, being told to baptize in the name of the "Father, Son, and Holy Spirit." In no way does this ordering indicate a lessening in divinity or power, but it is simply the way Christ communicated a simple truth that our limited minds struggle to understand.

> We neither say that the Holy Spirit is unbegotten—for we know one Unbegotten and one Beginning of beings, the Father of our Lord Jesus Christ—nor do we say that he is begotten; for in the Tradition of the Faith we have been taught that there is one Only-Begotten. We have been taught that the Spirit of Truth proceeds from the Father, and we confess that he is uncreatedly from God. . . . We must add this also, that they must be shunned as evidently hostile to piety who overturn the order given us by the Lord and place the Son before the Father, and the Holy Spirit before the Son. Indeed, we must preserve unaltered and inviolate the order which we have received from the very words of the Lord when he said, "Going forth, make disciples of all nations, baptizing them in the name of the Father and of the Son and of the Holy Spirit."[4]

The Father begets the Son in the Holy Spirit, for the Spirit is the union, the Love, between the eternal Lover and the Beloved Son. Yet Jesus instructs us how to baptize because He has taken the Jewish custom of circumcision for Hebrew boys and opened

---

4 *The Transcript of Faith Dictated by the Most Holy Basil and Signed by Eusthathius, Bishop of Sebaste* in 373, in *The Faith of the Early Fathers*, vol. 2, trans. W. A. Jurgens (Collegeville, MN: The Liturgical Press, 1979), 5 (no. 917).

this "basis" and "gateway" into God's chosen people for all: "Holy Baptism is the basis of the whole Christian life, the gateway to life in the Spirit (*vitae spiritualis ianua*), and the door which gives access to the other sacraments. Through Baptism we are freed from sin and reborn as sons of God; we become members of Christ, are incorporated into the Church and made sharers in her mission: 'Baptism is the sacrament of regeneration through water in the word'" (CCC 1213).

Pay attention to all that Baptism gives us. According to this particular section of the *Catechism*, Baptism empowers the new Christian with five new realities: (1) a life in the Spirit, (2) entry into all the other sacraments of the Church, (3) purification from the stain of original sin, (4) a rebirth realized as divine adoption, (5) incorporation into the Body of Christ, and (6) a vocation in Christ's Church to live out one's mission on earth.

As the waters were among the first of natural creatures, Baptism is the first of the gifts of supernatural regeneration. It is pure gift, God's generosity extended into the most primal of His creatures, where water meets life. And what could symbolize the free nature of this grace better than infant Baptism? The Church Fathers were in agreement that "the custom, all the same, of mother Church in baptizing babies is never on any account to be spurned nor in any way to be set aside as superfluous; nor should one believe at all that it is anything but an apostolic tradition."[5] Or as a liturgical guide from the early third century instructs:

> At cockcrow prayer shall be made over the water. The stream shall flow through the baptismal tank or pour into it from above when there is no scarcity of water; but if there is a scarcity, whether constant or sudden, then use whatever water you can find. They shall remove their clothing. And first baptize the little ones; if they can speak for themselves, they shall do so; if not, their parents or other relatives shall speak for them. Then baptize the men, and last of all the women; they

[5] Augustine, *The Literal Meaning of Genesis* 10.23.39, in *On Genesis*, trans. Edmund Hill (Hyde Park, NY: New City Press, 2004), 423.

> must first loosen their hair and put aside any gold or silver ornaments that they were wearing: let no one take any alien thing down to the water with them.
>
> At the hour set for the baptism the bishop shall give thanks over oil and put it into a vessel: this is called the "oil of thanksgiving". And he shall take other oil and exorcise it: this is called "the oil of exorcism." The anointing is performed by a presbyter. A deacon shall bring the oil of exorcism, and shall stand at the presbyter's left hand; and another deacon shall take the oil of thanksgiving, and shall stand at the presbyter's right hand. Then the presbyter, taking hold of each of those about to be baptized, shall command him to renounce, saying: "I renounce thee, Satan, and all thy servants and all thy works." And when he has renounced all these, the presbyter shall anoint him with the oil of exorcism, saying: "Let all spirits depart far from thee." Then, after these things, let him give him over to the presbyter who baptizes, and let the candidates stand in the water, naked, a deacon going with them likewise. And when he who is being baptized goes down into the water, he who baptizes him, putting his hand on him, shall say thus: "Dost thou believe in God, the Father Almighty?" And he who is being baptized shall say: "I believe."[6]

The Fathers knew that since Baptism led one on earth to the heavenly gate more directly, more swiftly, and more assuredly than any other rite, it was to be open to all. For all have contracted the contagion of Adam's original sin, and that is why Cyprian of Carthage even made the point that "no one is denied access to baptism

---

6 *The Apostolic Tradition* 21:16 [most often attributed to Hippolytus of Rome in the early 200's], in *The Apostolic Tradition of Hippolytus*, trans. Burton Scott Easton (Cambridge: Cambridge University Press, 1934), 45–46. The tradition of "deaconesses," simply Greek for "female helper," comes from this practice of accompanying naked adult women into the pool of baptism and was not ever an ordained position having to do with the sacrament of Holy Orders.

and grace. How much less reason is there then for denying it to an infant, who, being newly born, can have committed no sins."[7]

Baptism begins with the assent of parents and/or godparents (if the one to be baptized is a newborn) that this is their will for this person's soul. While a simple question, the sad truth behind this moment is that we in this fallen world are still rebellious children of Adam and Eve and are in dire need of the medicine of immortality. That is why the baptismal liturgy begins with the anointing of exorcism, claiming this person for the New Adam and Eve, Christ and Our Lady, alone: "Almighty and ever-living God, you sent your only Son into the world to cast out the power of Satan, spirit of evil, to rescue man from the kingdom of darkness, and bring him into the splendor of your kingdom of light. We pray for this child: set him (her) free from original sin, make him (her) a temple of your glory, and send your Holy Spirit to dwell with him (her). We ask this through Christ our Lord."

While *exorcism* is a term we do not hear much these days, the theology behind this moment is still in accord with the teaching of all the Church Fathers, even as the theology behind Baptism grew. Another constant is how this anointing and consequent Baptism removes one from the Old Adam to the New, Jesus.

Original sin has marred the intimacy God intended for His human race, but it need never be the final word. Baptism cleanses us of that rebellion and imparts the Holy Spirit into our souls, both the original sin from conception and any actual sins a later catechumen has inevitably committed. Again, the great exegete Origen makes clear how Baptism can never be repeated because it imparts an irremovable seal on the soul (what theologians call an "indelible mark"): "Let us also remember the sins we have committed, and that it is impossible to receive forgiveness of sins apart from baptism, that it is impossible according to the laws of the Gospel to be baptized

7 Cyprian, *Letter* 65.5, in *The Letters of St. Cyprian of Carthage*, vol. 3, Letters 55-66, trans. G. W. Clarke (Mahwah, NJ: The Newman Press, 1986), 112.

again with water and the Spirit for the forgiveness of sins, and that the baptism of martyrdom has been given to us."[8]

But as persecutions against the Church grew, a new sense of baptism—that by one's blood of martyrdom—came into view. Those who through no fault of their own had not yet received the Baptism of water were considered Christian through the blood that gushed forth from them in imitation of the crucified Christ:

> If any man receive not Baptism, he has not salvation; except only Martyrs, who even without the water receive the kingdom. For when the Saviour, in redeeming the world by His Cross, was pierced in the side, He shed forth blood and water; that men, living in times of peace, might be baptized in water, and, in times of persecution, in their own blood. For martyrdom also the Saviour is wont to call a baptism, saying, "Can you drink the cup which I drink, and be baptized with the baptism that I am baptized with?" (Mk 10:38). And the Martyrs confess, by "being made a spectacle unto the world, and to Angels, and to men" (1 Cor 4:9); and you will soon confess:—but it is not yet the time for you to hear of this.[9]

The sacrament of Baptism is so essential to salvation that it was extended to the "unbaptized" who died for Christ. The water and the blood become one in the cleansing and preparing the soul for its heavenly reward.

Another extension of Baptism is the Church's uninterrupted teaching that as long as one is baptized (1) with water and (2) in "the name of the Father, Son, and Holy Spirit," even if administered by a heretic or atheist, that person is validly baptized.

> From that time at which our Savior said, "If anyone is not reborn of water and the Spirit, he cannot enter into the kingdom of heaven" (Jn 3:5), no one can, without the Sacrament of

---

8 Origen, *An Exhortation to Martyrdom* §30, in *Origen*, trans. Rowan Greer (New York: Paulist Press, 1979), 61.

9 Cyril of Jerusalem, *Catechetical Lectures* 3:10, New Advent translation, https://www.newadvent.org/fathers/310103.htm.

> Baptism, except those who, in the Catholic Church, without Baptism, pour out their blood for Christ, receive the kingdom of heaven and life eternal. Anyone who receives the Sacrament of Baptism, whether in the Catholic Church or in a heretical or schismatic one, receives the whole Sacrament—but salvation, which is the strength of the Sacrament, he will not have, if he has had that Sacrament outside the Catholic Church. He must, therefore, return to the Church, not so that he might receive again the Sacrament of Baptism, which no one dare repeat in any baptized person, but so that he may receive eternal life in Catholic society, for the obtaining of which no one is suited, who, even with the Sacrament of Baptism, remains estranged from the Catholic Church.[10]

This distinction between the validity of the sacrament and its fruitfulness in the life of its recipient is essential and something to which we can all relate. The sacraments are not magic in that God refuses to let them work apart from our cooperation. We must desire the power of that grace and constantly look for ways to put that power into action. How often we have received the Body and Blood of Christ, how often we have had our souls thoroughly cleansed, and simply go on with our day as if nothing ever really happened!

After the initial anointing with the Oil of Catechumens and the prayer of exorcism follows the watery baptism itself. At this point, the priest or deacon will bless the font and invoke God's holy name over one of His first creations, the waters:

> Father . . . in baptism we use your gift of water, which you have made a rich symbol of the grace you give us in this sacrament. At the very dawn of creation your Spirit breathed on the waters, making them the wellspring of all holiness. The waters of the great flood you made a sign of the waters of baptism, that make an end of sin and a new beginning of goodness. Through the waters of the Red Sea you led Israel out of slavery, to be an image of God's holy people, set free from sin by baptism. In

10 Fulgentius of Ruspe, *The Rule of Faith* §43, in *The Faith of the Early Fathers*, vol. 3, 297.

the waters of the Jordan your Son was baptized by John and anointed with the Spirit.

And since freedom of will is at the heart of all our reception of Christ's care, after a recitation of the Creed we just examined last week, the adult to be baptized or the parents and godparents speaking for the newborn are asked: Is it your will that N. should be baptized in the faith of the Church, which we have all professed with you?

The parents and godparents must respond: "It is." Then the celebrant immerses three times or pours water on the head of the baptized, praying: "N., I baptize you in the name of the Father, and of the Son, and of the Holy Spirit." Oftentimes at this moment, there is some applause and forms of celebration, but God is not done yet. At this point, it is true that the Church has received a new Christian, but there is one more essential part of the rite: the anointing of the Holy Spirit.

This anointing is with the Oil of Sacred Chrism, from the same stock a bishop uses at priestly ordination and during the sacrament of Confirmation. This sealing marks the Holy Spirit's indwelling, and henceforth, this baptized person will never again be alone. From this moment on, the Holy Spirit is as active as this free-willed person allows, sharing in the "triple office" of Christ's priesthood, prophecy, and kingship. To be a priest is to offer the sacrifice of this person's daily life up to his or her heavenly father; to be a prophet is to speak the liberating words of the Gospel and to witness to the power of Jesus Christ in the world; to be a king is to rule over one's own choices and not to be led by one's fallen desires like a brute animal.

This final moment of the sacrament of Baptism then has the celebrant praying: "God the Father of our Lord Jesus Christ has freed you from sin, given you a new birth by water and the Holy Spirit, and welcomed you into his holy people. He now anoints you with the chrism of salvation. As Christ was anointed Priest, Prophet, and King, so may you live always as a member of his body, sharing everlasting life."

The child is anointed on the crown of the head with the Oil of Sacred Chrism in silence.

> And about your laughing at me and calling me Christian, you know not what you are saying. First, because that which is anointed is sweet and serviceable, and far from contemptible. For what ship can be serviceable and seaworthy, unless it be first caulked [anointed]? Or what castle or house is beautiful and serviceable when it has not been anointed? And what man, when he enters into this life or into the gymnasium, is not anointed with oil? And what work has either ornament or beauty unless it be anointed and burnished? Then the air and all that is under heaven is in a certain sort anointed by light and spirit; and are you unwilling to be anointed with the oil of God? Wherefore we are called Christians on this account, because we are anointed with the oil of God.[11]

> Do you not know that the imposition of hands after Baptism for an invocation of the Holy Spirit is the custom of the Churches? Do you demand to know where it is written? In the Acts of the Apostles. And even if it had not the authority of Scripture the consent of the whole world in this matter would confer on it the force of precept.[12]

We are Christians because we too have been anointed with the chrism of the priesthood of Jesus Christ, Son by nature, we by grace. The first followers of Jesus were originally known by outsiders as people of *the Way* (cf. Acts 9:2), but soon their focal point of Jesus alone earned them the name *Christian* (cf. Acts 11:26), and not soon thereafter *Catholic* by Saint Ignatius of Antioch around 107: "Where the bishop is to be seen, there let all his people be; just as wherever Jesus Christ is present, we have the Catholic Church."[13] The Christian thus shares in the messianic roles of the Christ, not as a lone

---

11 Theophilus of Antioch, *To Autolycus* 1.12 (A.D. 181), New Advent translation, https://www.newadvent.org/fathers/02041.htm.

12 St. Jerome, *Dialogue Against the Luciferians* 8, New Advent translation, https://www.newadvent.org/fathers/3005.htm.

13 Ignatius of Antioch, *Letter to the Smyrneans* §8, in *Early Christian Writings*, trans. Maxwell Staniforth (New York: Penguin Books, 1987), 103.

individual but as a new member of a body pertaining to the whole (what *Catholic* means, "according to the whole") of Jesus's Church.

Accordingly, this chrismation is administered as the beginning of a Christian's life, later to be strengthened and solidified by the sacrament of Confirmation. This act grants us access to Christ the High (and only) Priest. That is why Theophilus in the second century has to defend the name of those who claim eternal salvation through the administration of oil—the mark of strength and preparation for battle, an ornamentation of the beautiful and a source of merriment and joy as well. We are called "Christians" and not Patrissians (after the Father) or Spiritualists (after the Holy Spirit) because we have been chrismed with the same holy oil as the Christ, the Messiah.

According to Jerome a couple centuries later, the explicit connection between this chrismation and the invocation of the Holy Spirit into the soul of the newly baptized is made all too clear. Thereafter comes the touching of the baptized's mouth and ears in order that he or she will hear the Gospel rightly and proclaim the truth openly (recalling Jesus's "Ephphetha Prayer" at Mk 7:34). Those present pray an Our Father and receive a final blessing. But what is truly awesome to see is how this rite was portrayed so wonderfully by the Church Fathers.

Where have you misused your ears? Where do you misuse your mouth? When you were baptized, these senses were consecrated for the Lord!

When you place your hand in a holy water font, do you pray for the original graces of Baptism?

Do you ever pray for your parents and godparents?

Are you comfortable praying and going to Mass with people of different life situations than yourself? Can you see how the Spirit acts in ways and in communities very foreign to your own?

Is there anyone among your family or friends you feel compelled to talk to about baptizing a child of theirs? Has the Faith fallen into disuse in your family circle?

Saint Augustine, preaching to the newly baptized in North Africa around the year 400, likens what we just experienced to a new Christian's becoming the Eucharist for the world. The baptismal font and the altar's sacrifice are always linked in the best theologians: we are baptized not only to receive but to become like Christ!

So, imagine the scene: It is the Easter Vigil, a dark night in ancient Carthage, and the famous bishop scripts his sermon to capitalize on the fact that the newly baptized are allowed to be present for the Eucharist for the first time. They were surely instructed in the Eucharistic Mystery during their time of formation (today's RCIA programs), but now they see the actual bread and wine, naturally eager to see what might happen next. The bishop of Hippo takes this opportunity to explain that what the baptized just underwent in the sacrament of Baptism is exactly what Jesus Christ does in the sacrament of the Eucharist. That is, Jesus Christ comes to us chosen, sanctified, broken, and given as both priest and victim.

Augustine continues, explaining that a sacrament should be understood as a deeper reality underlying what we are allowed to sense through our experiences. Accordingly, we might see only a cup and some bread, but we are actually encountering the very Body and Blood of Jesus Christ. The baptized must therefore also imitate this sacramental holiness: becoming what they receive and being transformed in ways not always obvious to the visible eye.

Let us quote this brief homily almost in full, appreciating the various ways Augustine explains the Easter mysteries: the beholding of the Eucharistic elements, the identification of Christ's historical body and His Eucharistic body, and the invitation to the faithful to see the mystery of their own consecration on the altar of sacrifice, for them, too, to become the Body of Christ:

> What you can see on the altar, you also saw last night; but what it was, what it meant, of what great reality it contained the sacrament, you had not yet heard. So what you can see, then, is bread and a cup; that's what even your eyes tell you; but as far as your faith asks to be instructed about, the bread is the body of Christ, the cup the blood of Christ. . . .
>
> The reason these things, brothers and sisters, are called sacraments is that in them one thing is seen, another is to be understood. What can be seen has a bodily appearance, what is to be understood provides spiritual fruit. So if you want to understand the body of Christ, listen to the Apostle Paul telling the faithful: "You, though, are the body of Christ and its members" (1 Cor. 12.27). So if it's you that are the body of Christ and its members, it's the mystery meaning you that has been placed on the Lord's table; what you receive is the mystery that means you! It is to what you are that reply "Amen," and by so replying you express your assent. What you hear, you see, is "The body of Christ," you answer "Amen." So be a member of the body of Christ, in order to make that "Amen" true.
>
> Remember that bread is not made from one grain, but from many. When you were being exorcised, it's as though you were being ground. When you were baptized it's as though you were mixed into dough. When you received the fire of the

> Holy Spirit, it's as though you were baked. Be what you can see, and receive what you are.[14]

If you are the "body of Christ" (1 Cor 12) when you receive the "Body of Christ," could you pray over your life in terms of the four verbs of the Mass: Jesus takes bread, blesses it, breaks it, and gives it?

In my life, I feel most "taken" or chosen when I think of _____.

In my life, I feel most blessed by _______________.

In my life, I feel broken when I think of _______________.

Yet, in this brokenness, Jesus has finally been able to give me away, obvious by ______________.

Are you able to see the mystery of your own life's story on the altar at Mass, a gift to the Father for the salvation of the world, in which He has intentionally placed you?

> Before beginning a second life, one must put an end to the first. . . . The Lord who gives us life also gave us the baptismal covenant, which contains an image of both death and life. The image of death is fulfilled in the water, and the Spirit gives us the pledge of life. . . . The water receives our body as a tomb,

---

14 Augustine, *Sermon* 272, in *Sermons III/7 (230-272B)*, trans. Edmund Hill (New Rochelle, NY: New City Press, 1993), 300–1.

> and so becomes an image of death, while the Spirit pours in life-giving power, renewing in souls which were dead in sin the life they first possessed. This is what it means to be born again of water and of Spirit. . . . If there is any grace in the water, it does not come from the nature of the water, but from the Holy Spirit's presence there, since baptism is not a removal of dirt from the body, but an appeal to God for a clear conscience.[15]

What would a "clear conscience" look like for you?

If the Spirit does in fact promise "new life," what would that look like for you? What practical changes might that invite you to make?

As the Church matured, more and more theology was devoted to the sacrament of Baptism, becoming more and more explicit regarding exactly what happens. To become a member of the Body of Christ requires a bond, a source of union between Christian and Christ, and this is the Holy Spirit's role. The Spirit is the person of the Trinity who lifts us out of this world and gives us the power to become children of heaven. As the Trinity's eternal Love between the Lover and Beloved, it belongs to the nature of the Spirit to bind people in union, and this is precisely what occurs at Baptism.

The wholeness the Spirit gives came to be known in terms of three sets of graces. That is, as the theology informing the sacrament of Baptism developed over time, the Church's theologians began to

---

15 Basil, *On the Holy Spirit* 15.35, trans. David Anderson (Crestwood, NY: St. Vladimir's Seminary Press, 1980), 58–59.

understand Baptism as how we become infused with virtues, gifts, and the fruits of the Holy Spirit. The first are the three theological virtues of faith, hope, and charity (cf. 1 Thes 1:3, 5:8; 1 Cor 13:13). Traditionally, faith is what unites us to God and enables us to assent to all that God has revealed. Hope is the virtue "with wings," as the ancients used to say. Hope unites us to our truest selves, allowing us to pilgrim through this earthly journey with the unassailable confidence of God's loving care. Regardless of how we might feel on any given day, hope assures that Christ is ours and we are His: "My lover belongs to me and I to him" (Sg 2:16). Hope, then, is perfected by charity, the love that binds us to God and neighbor. Charity not only longs for the eternal good of the other but also to be in the other's presence forever. Benevolence and union are thus the two key characteristics of true love. Together, these gifts infused in the soul at Baptism both transform and elevate, transforming us into God's children and elevating us to live above human fallenness and in accord with the promptings of the Holy Spirit: "The theological virtues are the foundation of Christian moral activity; they animate it and give it its special character. They inform and give life to all the moral virtues. They are infused by God into the souls of the faithful to make them capable of acting as his children and of meriting eternal life. They are the pledge of the presence and action of the Holy Spirit in the faculties of the human being. There are three theological virtues: faith, hope, and charity" (CCC 1813).

The theological virtues place reality on a wholly different plane. Although they inhabit the same time and place, the Christian and non-Christian inhabit two very different worlds. Without the theological virtues and the Crucified and Risen Christ from where they both originate and end, everything collapses into the few decades we spend on this earth. As a result, death is nothing other than disappointment, tragedy has no salvation, and even the brighter days of living are clouded over by lack of ultimate purpose and the inevitability of absolute nothingness once these days are past. Only the light of Jesus Christ can shed a purifying light on the darkness of death and reveal it for what can be: the necessary step toward our eternal joy in the Beatific Vision.

Take, for example, the loss of a job or the inevitable death of a loved one. Where one apart from Christ would only see setback and disappointment, one in the Spirit can meet and tend to the rejected Christ, the dying Christ. Faith, hope, and love reconfigure what the world considers only loss (because it is that, no doubt) into an encounter with a God who first walked this costly path of the world, the spurning of supposed friends, and the fateful moment of a last breath. While these experiences are real and painful for everyone, such experiences for the Christian can become invitations and blessed opportunities. This does not take away the hard reality of sin and depletion, but it consecrates these tender times, uniting our life's most precious moments with Jesus Christ, who has descended with us only to defeat all that keeps us from the Father. "For faith in our teacher continues firm, assuring us that there is only one who is truly God and that we should really love God always, since he alone is Father; and that consequently we should hope to receive something more and to learn from God that he is good and possesses unlimited riches, and eternal kingdom, and infinite knowledge."[16]

> What is there that we can hope for without believing in it? . . . The fact that we do not see either the things we believe in or those we hope for makes not seeing a feature that faith and hope have in common. . . . And now what should I say about love? Without it faith has no value. But hope cannot exist without love. The apostle James says, *Even the demons believe—and shudder* (Jas 2:19), yet they do not hope or love but rather fear that which we hope for and love, believing that it will come about. That is why the apostle Paul approves and recommends *the faith that works through love* (Gal 5:6), which cannot exist without hope. So love cannot exist without hope nor hope without love, nor can either exist without faith.[17]

---

16 Irenaeus of Lyons, *Against the Heresies* 2.28.3, in *Against the Heresies* (Book 2), trans. Dominic Unger (Mahwah, NJ: The Newman Press, 2012), 88.

17 Augustine of Hippo, *The Enchiridion on Faith, Hope, and Charity*, 2.8, in

How do you see the role of faith in your life? Do you distinguish between the Christian sense of faith as trusting God's revelation and the more secular sense of believing something will happen?

How do you see the role of hope in your life? Of all Christ's promises, for what do you find yourself hoping the most?

How do you see the role of love in your life? Do you see your love of friend and God as the same love or do you distinguish between a love you think is Christian and one that is natural?

At Baptism, one also receives the seven gifts of the Holy Spirit. The gifts are first found in Scripture, in one of the prophecies of Isaiah, which Christians have always read as foreshadowing the coming of Jesus. These gifts are signs indicating that one is living in the Holy Spirit. Although found naturally and perfectly in Jesus, He "sprouts from the stump of Jesse" in order to share these gifts with those humble enough to follow Him: "But a shoot shall sprout from the stump of Jesse, and from his roots a bud shall blossom. The spirit of the Lord shall rest upon him: a spirit of wisdom and of understanding, a spirit of counsel and of strength, a spirit of knowledge and of fear of the Lord, and his delight shall be the fear of the Lord. Not by appearance shall he judge, nor by hearsay shall he decide" (Is 11:1–3).

On Christian Belief, trans. Bruce Harbert (Hyde Park, NY: New City Press, 2005), 276–77.

In time, this passage came to be interpreted in light of the New Testament, and the early Christians thus saw how the gifts of the Holy Spirit should be enumerated and grouped as these seven, as the last gift can be as easily interpreted "fear" as "piety" in Hebrew:

- Wisdom
- Understanding
- Knowledge
- Counsel
- Fortitude
- Piety
- Fear of the Lord

These seven gifts of the Holy Spirit, according to the *Catechism of the Catholic Church* "belong in their fullness to Christ, Son of David. They complete and perfect the virtues of those who receive them. They make the faithful docile in readily obeying divine inspirations." This insight is then illuminated by three Bible verses, indicating exactly what the fruits are meant to do: "Let your good spirit lead me on a level path (Ps 143:10). For all who are led by the Spirit of God are sons and daughters of God (Rom 8:14).... If children, then heirs, heirs of God and fellow heirs with Christ (Rom 8:17)" (CCC 1831).

The gifts are obviously intended to further our adoption into the Father's perfect love, His eternal embrace. They open our otherwise stony hearts to be led by the Spirit, securing us in the Father's care and thus transforming how we live during our time on earth. When we begin to live out these gifts, we begin to live more docilely under the promptings of the Spirit.

The virtues may be the beginning of the Christian life, but the gifts deepen and intensify the virtues. Wisdom, Understanding, Counsel, and Knowledge perfect the gifts of the intellect, penetrating the truths of the Faith and empowering us mortals to begin to think, see, and speak in unison with the Creator. "Listen, human creature:

what my scripture says, I myself say. . . . What you see through my Spirit, I see, just as what you say through my Spirit, I say."[18]

The Spirit's gift of fortitude unites our status as pilgrims with Christ who has already endured the ills of this life, enabling us to "persevere in running the race that lies before us while keeping our eyes fixed on Jesus, the leader and perfecter of faith" (Heb 12:1b–2a). Now one with the saints, those who live in accord with the Spirit can be ensured that Christ not only suffered for them but is even now suffering in and even as them. Taunted with cruel martyrdom, the Christian slave girl Felicity advised the guards before the bloody spectacle as they were mocking her, "You who are in such suffering now, what will you do when you are thrown to the beasts, which you despised when you refused to sacrifice?" And turning to them, Felicity replied, "Now it is I that suffer what I suffer; but then there will be another in me, who will suffer for me, because I also am about to suffer for him."[19]

Piety and Fear of the Lord indicate that one judges rightly the awesomeness of God and lives a life worthy of being counted among the Lord's chosen. This convergence is prayed beautifully in today's Mass (Eucharistic Prayer II) when the priest says on all our behalf, "Therefore, as we celebrate the memorial of his Death and Resurrection, we offer you, Lord, the Bread of life and the Chalice of salvation, giving thanks that you have held us worthy to be in your presence and minister to you. Humbly we pray that, partaking of the Body and Blood of Christ, we may be gathered into one by the Holy Spirit." Piety means fulfilling one's religious duties, and fear of the Lord means doing so with humility, realizing that none of us are naturally worthy to be in God's presence, "Lord, I am not worthy to receive you, but only say the word and I shall be healed" (cf. Mt 8:8).

Yet here you are most likely saved in God's presence, christened, and receiving His Sacred Body and Blood. This is because Jesus

---

18 Augustine, *Confessions*, 13.29.44, trans. Maria Boulding (Hyde Park, NY: New City Press, 1997), 374.

19 *The Passion of Perpetua and Felicity* 5.2, trans. New Advent, https://www.newadvent.org/fathers/0324.htm.

is the One in you who makes you worthy; His presence is what elevates you into another son or daughter of His Father; He is the one who has made the saints your siblings! In this merriment and confidence, stop now and give God thanks for all He is doing in you.

How is God acting in you? Through you? As you?

How do you live out the virtues of faith, hope, and love in your life?

What gift of the Holy Spirit most resonates with you, an obvious trait in your life?

Which gift seems furthest away from where you are today?

Perfecting these virtues and gifts are the twelve fruits of the Holy Spirit. These are so called because they are the foretastes of what the Christian life is all about. When we allow ourselves to live in accord with the fruits while on earth, we are experiencing what heaven will be like forever.

The fruits show us who we are meant to be: fully formed children of the Father who no longer teeter between right and wrong but are wholly intent on living the Christ-life. But when we are honest with ourselves, each of us knows that the war is still on—that ancient war in our souls between good and evil, between God and all that chooses to dwell far from God. So while the fruits truly are perfections, they do not automatically erase our imperfections but aim to strengthen our free will to be open to the inspirations of the Holy Spirit. That is, throughout all of these reflections on the Holy Spirit's life in ours, we are never robbed of our free choice and our humanity. We remain able to accept God's grace more and more, but only if we so desire. Perhaps that is why Saint Paul contrasts the two possible ways of living our lives so strongly:

> Now the works of the flesh are obvious: immorality, impurity, licentiousness, idolatry, sorcery, hatreds, rivalry, jealousy, outbursts of fury, acts of selfishness, dissensions, factions, occasions of envy, drinking bouts, orgies, and the like. I warn you, as I warned you before, that those who do such things will not inherit the kingdom of God. In contrast, the fruit of the Spirit is love, joy, peace, patience, kindness, generosity, faithfulness, gentleness, self-control. Against such there is no law. Now those who belong to Christ [Jesus] have crucified their flesh with its passions and desires. If we live in the Spirit, let us also follow the Spirit. (Gal 5:19–25)

The traditional list of the twelve fruits of the Spirit are therefore:

- Charity
- Joy
- Peace
- Generosity
- Gentleness
- Faithfulness
- Patience
- Kindness
- Goodness
- Modesty
- Self-control
- Chastity

The biblical teaching for the twelve Fruits of the Holy Spirit is clearly opposed to the rotten fruits of the spirit of the world, the spirit of the times.

How do you feel when you are tempted to entertain (or in fact do so) the "works of the flesh" Paul outlines here? Does living apart from the Spirit make you morose, sad, and anxious?

What do you do when you fall in this area?

Which of these fruits are you most drawn to and why?

Sin robs us of the "love, joy, and peace" for which God has created us. But what is really scary is that some people are so accustomed to living in fear, anxiety, and feeling disconnected to anything, to anyone, they settle for the rotten fruit of their self-imposed tiny world. But the Spirit's indwelling at Baptism has lifted us out of the world, allowing us to die to such temptations and live a heavenly life, if only we are willing to die with Jesus and then ascend to the Father with Him.

> How can we become like him in his death? By being buried with him in baptism. What kind of burial is it, and what is gained from such imitation? First, it is necessary that the old way of life be terminated, and this is impossible unless a man

> is born again. . . . The image of death is fulfilled in the water, and the Spirit gives us the pledge of life. Therefore it is clear why water is associated with the Spirit: because of baptism's dual purpose. On the one hand, the body of sin is destroyed, that it may never bear fruit for death. On the other hand, we are made to live by the Spirit, and bear fruit in holiness. The water receives our body as a tomb, and so becomes the image of death, while the Spirit pours in life-giving power, renewing in souls which were dead in sin the life they first possessed.[20]

The threefold immersion or the thrice outpouring of baptismal water symbolizes the three days of death God endured for our waywardness. But Baptism is not about simply salvaging a sunken ship; it is about giving that ship the sleekest sails in the fleet. That is what the gifts do: enable us not to trudge through the Christian life but to swiftly and joyfully fulfill the commandments and live life in the Spirit. On account of this new life, we have been made "good," but God is "Goodness" and continually looks for ways to share that life with us: "But let us see whether the Holy Spirit has goodness, since he is the source and principle of goodness. For just as the Father and the Son have goodness, so also the Holy Spirit has goodness. This the Apostle also taught when he said: 'But the fruit of the Spirit is peace, charity, joy, patience, goodness' (Gal 5:22). But who doubts that he is good whose fruit is goodness? For 'a good tree yields good fruit' (Mt 7:17)."[21]

What is important to stress at the beginning of this week is that the Holy Spirit is one and He is ultimately love. Yet this love comes to us in various ways, as the sun in the sky is one but can be refracted and received in a myriad of ways depending on where we stand or what we wear. The graces of the Holy Spirit are like this: although one, the Spirit comes to us and affects us in so many varied ways.

---

20 Basil of Caesarea, *On the Holy Spirit,* 15.35, pp. 58–59.

21 Ambrose, *The Holy Spirit,* Bk 1, ch. 5.69, *Ambrose: Theological and Dogmatic Works,* trans. Roy J. Deferrari (Washington, DC: Catholic University of America Press, 1962), 60.

At Baptism, each of us underwent our own personal Pentecost: the Holy Spirit descended and began to live personally and uniquely in each of our souls. He was released through the words of Jesus, echoing in every Rite of Baptism, "I baptize you in the name of the Father, and of the Son, and of the Holy Spirit." Chances are your baptism occurred many years ago, but that should be no reason to think of it as an event only in the past. Every Church you enter has holy water available—in the large baptistery or in the smaller holy water fonts on the doorposts as you make that symbolic move from "secular" into "sacred" space. Find where you can buy some plastic holy water bottles and ask your pastor to fill those up—bless yourselves at home, bless your children, and use such sacramentals to consecrate the place where you pray, the place you love, the place you argue and ask forgiveness! For the holy waters of Baptism not only cleanse us of sin, they transform us into extensions of Christ Himself.

> This is what happens with us, whose model the Lord made himself. When we are baptized, we are enlightened; being enlightened, we become adopted sons and daughters; becoming adopted sons and daughters, we are made perfect; and becoming perfect, we are made divine. "I have said," it is written, "you are gods and all of you sons and daughters of the Most High" (Ps 81:6). This ceremony is called "free gift," "enlightenment," "perfection," and "cleansing"—"cleansing" because through it we are completely purified of our sins; "free gift" because by it the punishments due to our sins is remitted; "enlightenment," since by it we behold the wonderful holy light of salvation, that is, it enables us to see God clearly; finally we call it "perfection" as needing nothing further, for what does he need who possesses the knowledge of God?[22]

---

[22] Clement of Alexandria, *Christ the Educator of Little Ones* 1.6.26, in *Christ the Educator*, trans. Simon Wood (Washington, DC: Catholic University of America Press, 2008), 26.

Do you have any memories or any old photographs of your baptism? Who was your priest or deacon; who are your godparents? Do you pray for them?

What do you pray as you dip your fingers into a holy water font? Do you ask for the grace to live out your baptismal vocation to become a saint?

How do you personally understand being cleansed, being illumined, being godly?

Week 4

The Holy Spirit and Sin: Conviction

The fourth Week of Easter joyfully begins with Good Shepherd Sunday. The Gospel comes from:

> John 10:1–10,
> John 10:11–18, or
> John 10:27–30.

The theme here is that regardless how much one has sinned, the Good Shepherd will drop everything and go after him. The world thinks of love as being drawn to that which is beautiful or handsome, where there is success and promise. The love of the Good Shepherd (who is Love) is the exact opposite: He pursues the lost, those who feel ashamed or unloved. He drops all the "perfect" ninety-nine (as if there were such a thing) and seeks out the abused and alienated one.

The battle between good and evil runs throughout this Gospel, the true Shepherd versus robbers and marauders. As much as we might love sin, it does not love us. It entices and beckons but only to destroy through momentary pleasure. Sin defaces and robs us of our unique glory. No group is as wildly diverse as the saints; the great sinners are the ones who always seem so much alike.

In his unmatchable letters between the devil and his nephew lurking on earth, C. S. Lewis puts this contrast as only he can. The enemy here of course is our loving Father in heaven, "He," so disrespectfully depicted:

> He really does want to fill the universe with a lot of loathsome little replicas of Himself—creatures whose life, on its miniature scale, will be qualitatively like His own, not because He has absorbed them but because their wills freely conform to His. We want cattle who can finally become food; He wants servants who can finally become sons. We want to suck in, He wants to give out. We are empty and would be filled; He is full and flows over. Our war aim is a world in which Our Father Below has drawn all other beings into himself: the Enemy wants a world full of beings united to Him but still distinct.[1]

Because we are made in God's image and likeness, the more we become like God, the more we become the "best version" of ourselves. This is why our relationship with Jesus Christ is not something added on to our human nature but is in fact the heart of what it means to be human, to be in a deifying union with Love Himself. For this we have been created, and apart from this, we shall become nothing other than "cattle" and "food."

The Good Shepherd of course knows this, and that is how He can pursue us without any harm to our identity or humanity. The God-made-man is now out to make men and women godly, to effect a union between the dying dissipation our sins have wrought and the perfect wholeness God alone can offer. That is why Christ has come as one of us, for only God can heal and only a dying man needs healing, and so the Son of God comes to live, to die, and then to rise from the dead, sending His Holy Spirit to all who kneel before that cross. "I am the good shepherd. A good shepherd lays down his life for the sheep" (Jn 10:11). This "lying down" is how the Good Shepherd makes room for all sinners in His own wounds. What is left is for those sinners now to quit resisting the salvation

---

1 C. S. Lewis, *The Screwtape Letters*, no. 8.

offered through the cross. On the contrary, the cross melts the hardest of hearts, making corresponding room for the Spirit of God to dwell ever more powerfully and personally.

Scripture makes it clear that the first moment of this mutual indwelling will be marked by the Holy Spirit convicting us of sin. This may sound a bit depressing, but it is actually good news. The root of *con-viction* is *to conquer* (*vincere* in Latin), and that is very different than *condemnation* (*damnare,* to damn, in Latin). "Since Easter, the Holy Spirit has proved 'the world wrong about sin,' i.e., proved that the world has not believed in him whom the Father has sent. But this same Spirit who brings sin to light is also the Consoler who gives the human heart grace for repentance and conversion" (CCC 1433). The Holy Spirit is our Comforter, our intimate Indweller, and He has come not to condemn us but to grant us victory. Yet, this does not mean that He stays away from the messy business of struggle and sin. If we allow Him to, He will name them and then give us the grace to defeat them. As Jesus teaches before His death:

> But I tell you the truth, it is better for you that I go. For if I do not go, the Advocate will not come to you. But if I go, I will send him to you. And when he comes he will convict the world in regard to sin and righteousness and condemnation: sin, because they do not believe in me; righteousness, because I am going to the Father and you will no longer see me; condemnation, because the ruler of this world has been condemned. "I have much more to tell you, but you cannot bear it now. But when he comes, the Spirit of truth, he will guide you to all truth. He will not speak on his own, but he will speak what he hears, and will declare to you the things that are coming. He will glorify me, because he will take from what is mine and declare it to you. (Jn 16:7–14)

The enfleshed Messiah left us two essential and eternal gifts: the continuation of His own physical presence in the Most Blessed Sacrament, alongside the sending of His Holy Spirit in a new and definitive way. Christ tells His followers, tells us, that the first thing the Spirt will do will be to "convict the world in regard to sin . . . because they do not believe in me."

Over your lifetime, what sin has "convicted" you the most mightily?

Do you make decisions based on what is true or on what is useful? Do you consider yourself a man or woman of truth?

When the Good Shepherd seeks you, where do you hide?

What might it mean for you to let the Good Shepherd have you, to surrender to Him and quit resisting His pursuit of love?

It would seem that "sin" in Jesus's mind here is therefore not only, and not even primarily, the malicious actions that you and I see committed (and commit ourselves) each and every day. Sin first and foremost is a cold indifference, a willing lack of belief, a turning away from trusting Jesus, the choice to live by our own lights than to place ourselves in the hands and heart of a loving God. This lack of faith is met by Jesus's most gracious promise that He will continue to teach and hopefully draw us all back into Himself. He shall do this through the Spirit, that divine Person who meets us anywhere and everywhere, at any time and in any state we find ourselves.

With the progress of Revelation, the reality of sin is also illuminated. Although to some extent the People of God in the Old Testament had tried to understand the pathos of the human condition in the light of the history of the fall narrated in Genesis, they could not grasp this story's ultimate meaning, which is revealed only in the light of the death and Resurrection of Jesus Christ. We must know Christ as the source of grace in order to know Adam as the source of sin. The Spirit-Paraclete, sent by the risen Christ, came to "convict the world concerning sin," by revealing him who is its Redeemer (CCC 388).

> The soul that has been judged worthy to share in the Spirit in his light, and has been illumined by the splendor of his ineffable glory becomes all light, all face, all eye, and no part of him remains any longer not filled with spiritual eyes and light. That means this one has no longer anything murky about him but is wholly Spirit and light, no longer having a reverse side but showing his face all around, for the indescribable beauty of Christ's glory and light have come to dwell in him. . . . This soul which has been illumined with the ineffable beauty and the glorious brightness of Christ's face has been filled with the Holy Spirit, and his soul has been found worthy to become the dwelling and temple of God.[2]

When we set out to complete a task, we first imagine what it is we want to do, what we need to accomplish it, and what might be the difficulties and setbacks. We then begin by eliminating all those obstacles as well as we can. We first weed the garden, say, before planting the seeds into the soil. After we clear debris and then go to work at whatever task we hope to finish, then we can sit back and enjoy the results. "Sanctifying grace is the gratuitous gift of his life that God makes to us; it is infused by the Holy Spirit into the soul to heal it of sin and to sanctify it" (CCC 2023). Grace first heals the soul of sin and then goes to work to sanctify it to the full. In

---

2 Pseudo-Macarius, *First Homily* §2, in *Roots of Christian Mysticism*, trans. Olivier Clément (Hyde Park, NY: New City Press, 1995), 248.

the middle of the third century, Origen likened the spiritual life to this three-fold method: *purgation* first, followed by *illumination*, and completed by *union* with the Trinity.

> Now the first of these manifests him—the healing of the sick and casting out of evil spirits, which could not be apart from the Spirit; and so does that breathing upon them after the Resurrection, which was clearly a divine inspiration; and so too the present distribution of the fiery tongues, which we are now commemorating. But the first manifested him indistinctly, the second more expressly, this present one more perfectly, since he is no longer present only in energy, but as we may say, substantially, associating with us, and dwelling in us. For it was fitting that as the Son had lived with us in bodily form—so the Spirit too should appear in bodily form; and that after Christ had returned to his own place, he should have come down to us—Coming because he is the Lord; Sent, because he is not a rival God. For such words no less manifest the Unanimity than they mark the separate Individuality.[3]

Purgation, Illumination, and Union are thus the three stages of the spiritual life used by many Church Fathers to gauge our growth in holiness. This tripartite order might prompt thoughts of the Catholic Mass. After a Triune introduction and greeting ("In the name of the Father, and of the Son, and of the Holy Spirit"), we begin with the Penitential Rite during which we bring God our sins and shortcomings from the previous liturgy. Is that not an amazing opening right there? Like the wounds of Christ earlier, bringing our hurts and pains to the Father is actually the beginning of worship, the start of right religion! It is our honest admittance that we are not yet who God has created us to be. "Be purified and you will see heaven in yourself. In yourself you will see angels and their brightness, and you will see their Master with them and in them. . . . This is your spiritual homeland, the place of the person whose soul has been purified is within. The sun that shines there is the light of the

---

3 Gregory of Nazianzus, *Oration* 41.11, New Advent translation, https://www.newadvent.org/fathers/310241.htm.

Trinity. The air breathed by the entering thoughts is the Holy Spirit, the Comforter. . . . That is the Kingdom of God hidden within us, according to the words of the Lord."[4]

After the Penitential Rite and Collect (the opening prayer which "collects" the major themes for that liturgical week), we receive the readings and homily. This is the illuminative, the place where God's Word is proclaimed and explained. Then comes the Liturgy of the Eucharist, the time for intimate union. Here is the consummation of the Catholic Mass, communion with God's own Body and Blood.

Realizing that union is the goal of the Christian life, to become godly just as God became human, we can now begin to outline the steps to grow in holiness as well as trace the sins that need to be purged from our lives in order to achieve that goal.

Do you ever prepare for Sunday Mass or are you always rushing just to make it in time?

Could you take time each week to pray over Mass readings?

Could you prepare a list of sins to bring to the Penitential Rite at the beginning of Mass?

Do you prepare to receive Jesus Christ in the Most Blessed Sacrament of the Eucharist? Are you able to get to Mass during

4 Isaac of Nineveh, *Ascetic Treatises* §43, in *Roots of Christian Mysticism*, 253.

the week or to make a Holy Hour at the times of Eucharist Adoration near you?

Scripture delineates two categories of sin: the "deadly" variety and those which are seemingly not so mortal. For the latter, the Church Fathers picked up on the Latin word for "forgivable" or "excusable," *venialis,* from which we get the term *venial sin.* It is the Evangelist John who first gives us this distinction: "If anyone sees his brother sinning, if the sin is not deadly, he should pray to God and he will give him life. This is only for those whose sin is not deadly. There is such a thing as deadly sin, about which I do not say that you should pray. All wrongdoing is sin, but there is sin that is not deadly" (1 Jn 5:16–17).

Once again, human common sense and Christian revelation converge: of course all wrongdoing is sinful and offensive to God, but there must be a difference between sins like murder and sins like growing impatient in a traffic jam. John therefore teaches us that some sin "is not deadly" and some which are "deadly sin." The former we call venial, and those, according to John, can be prayed over; for the latter, we use John's own term, *mortalis,* and for those one cannot seemingly simply pray away. In her wisdom, the Church has never outlined what exactly are "venial" and what are "mortal," for so much depends on the person's intention, the act itself, as well as the freedom and knowledge of the acting person. What may be a minor fault for one might actually be a mortal sin for one who commits such a deed only to offend God.

Not long after John wrote this, Christian thinkers tried to figure out what exactly constitutes a deadly sin. Tertullian, the third-century African strongman we met earlier, came up with the canonical number seven and included what we might think: murder and adultery and so on. By the end of the fourth century, however, an Eastern monk gave us the order that has more or less stayed in place since (although Evagrius originally had "8 Evil Thoughts"). Pope Gregory the Great thus reworked Evagrius's list a bit, Thomas Aquinas defined the sins, and Dante's *Inferno* enshrined hell's movement from lust to pride in unforgettable imagery.

One way to think of the deadly sins is a list that runs inversely to the ultimate virtue of charity. That is, if we are made for a union of love, pride is the worst of the deadly sins because the proud person cares about no one but him or herself. Envy comes next because at least the envious person realizes that he or she is not at the center of the world; there are still goods to pursue. The wrathful person goes out of him or herself even more, showing a certain vulnerability in their frustration. In the middle of the deadly sins is sloth, a sin that is neither hot nor cold (cf. Rv 3:15) but is a wandering among goods without any real purpose or plan. The final three sins are avarice, gluttony, and lust, indicating that very human need for goods outside of oneself.

COLD SINS	LUKEWARM SIN	HOT SINS
Pride	Sloth (Acedia in Greek)	Avarice (Greed)
Envy		Gluttony
Wrath		Lust

Pride is essentially thinking your talents and successes are yours and not gifts from God for the good of all. The sin of pride ranges from attributing perfections to yourself that you do not really possess (those little lies, putting on airs, etc.) to realizing you actually do have those gifts but wrongly believe you have them because you worked hard or somehow deserve them. The proud person says, "I am excellent at this or that because I practiced every day, because I studied really hard," while the humble person admits, "I am excellent at this or that because God has blessed me with loving parents, a healthy work ethic, sound health, and so on."

After an extended tour of the monastic East of the fifth century, John Cassian returned to France to report how the monks there made progress in holiness. Moving from least deadly to the worst sin of pride, Cassian notes that the "last combat is against the spirit of pride, which evil, although it is the latest in our conflict with our faults and stands last on the list, yet in beginning and in the order of time is the first: an evil beast that is most savage and more dreadful than all the former ones, chiefly trying those who are perfect, and devouring with its dreadful bite those who have almost attained the consummation of virtue."[5] It may be the last thing we ever have eradicated from our soul, but pride is the first, giving rise to all the other sins because the proud person thinks he or she is the arbiter of what is good and evil (cf. Gn 3:5).

Next comes envy, that stubborn unwillingness to allow others to enjoy God's goodness to them, also realized as an unwillingness to share our gifts with others (jealousy) or to destroy all gifts so no one can enjoy them (spite). Envious wrath saps the soul of all joy, especially the joy of gratitude. Thus the envious person is in a constant state of feeling offended or rebuffed, if not ignored.

> To such, no food is joyous, no drink can be cheerful. They are ever sighing, and groaning, and grieving; and since envy is never put off by the envious, the possessed heart is rent without intermission day and night. Other ills have their limit; and whatever wrong is done, is bounded by the completion of the crime. In the adulterer the offense ceases when the violation is perpetrated; in the case of the robber, the crime is at rest when the homicide is committed; and the possession of the booty puts an end to the rapacity of the thief; and the completed deception places a limit to the wrong of the cheat. Jealousy has no limit; it is an evil continually enduring, and a sin without end.[6]

As we descend down the list of the severity of capital sins, we can see how sins bring one out of himself. Pride is easy to conceal,

---

[5] John Cassian, *Institutes* 12.1, New Advent translation, https://www.newadvent.org/fathers/310241.htm.

[6] Cyprian, *On Jealousy and Envy* §10.7, New Advent translation, https://www.newadvent.org/fathers/050710.htm.

envy, we say, turns one "green," while wrath is manifested in very clear ways. Yet wrath is not the deadliest sin because it shows some vulnerability. There is a certain caring in showing another that he has broken your trust, a vulnerability in admitting that you have been hurt.

> To prefer nothing to the love of Christ.
> Not to carry anger into effect.
> Not to prolong the duration of one's wrath.
> Not to retain guile in one's heart.
> Not to make a false peace.
> Not to abandon charity.
> Not to swear, lest perchance one forswear.
> To utter only truth from heart and mouth.
> Not to return evil for evil.
> Not to do injury, but to suffer it patiently.
> To love enemies.
> Not to curse in return those who curse one, but rather to bless them.
> To bear persecution for righteousness.[7]

When do you feel proud? Is it a sense of self-accomplishment or a healthier sense of gratitude for God's giving you the grace to achieve this?

Do you worry too much about material possessions, money, retirement possibilities? Where do you find yourself feeling most envious?

---

[7] Benedict of Nursia, *The Rule* 4, *The Rule of St. Benedict*, trans. W. K. Lowther Clarke (London: S.P.C.K., 1931), 5.

Do you ever "snap" and use the Lord's name in vain or lash out and say things you instantly regret just moments later?

These are the three cold sins, and the three hot sins are to follow. Right in the middle is perhaps *the* sin of our times. While we all have a fairly good understanding of the other deadly sins, what may come as a shock is the Church Fathers' understanding of sloth. The Greek term *acedia* captures it better, meaning literally "without care." For this sin is not physical laziness as we might think but actually the opposite: being so busy and so given to wandering that the slothful person never keeps in mind what is of ultimate value. The soul afflicted with acedia therefore flits about from pursuit to pursuit. It is the sin of middle-age when the excitement of youth has worn off and the seriousness of impending mortality has not yet set in. Evagrius thus writes:

> The demon of acedia, which is also called the noonday demon, is the most burdensome of all the demons. It besets the monk at about the fourth hour (10 am) of the morning, encircling his soul until about the eighth hour (2 pm). First it makes the sun seem to slow down or stop moving, so that the day appears to be fifty hours long. Then it makes the monk keep looking out of his window and forces him to go bounding out of his cell to examine the sun to see how much longer it is to 3 o'clock, and to look round in all directions in case any of the brethren is there. Then it makes him hate the place and his way of life and his manual work. It makes him think that there is no charity left among the brethren; no one is going to come and visit him. If anyone has upset the monk recently, the demon throws this in too to increase his hatred. It makes him desire other places where he can easily find all that he needs and practice an easier, more convenient craft. After all, pleasing the Lord is not dependent on geography, the demon

> adds; God is to be worshipped everywhere. It joins to this the remembrance of the monk's family and his previous way of life, and suggests to him that he still has a long time to live, raising up before his eyes a vision of how burdensome the ascetic life is. So, it employs, as they say, every [possible] means to move the monk to abandon his cell and give up the race.[8]

Is this not the sin of our modern world where we are rewarded for multitasking? We are inundated with endless possibilities. We are stretched and have come to "need" such drama, a fast-paced world filled with novelty. We have become used to the fact that at the push of a button we are able to talk and see friends around the world; we all have way too many tabs open on our laptops at any one time; we all drive and text; we all equate downtime with failure. *The antidote to sloth is not more activity but less,* it is the need to slow down and prioritize one's life's commitments.

Later than the Church Fathers, the Medievals defined sloth as "the tendency to wander." Do you find yourself multitasking to the detriment of doing any one thing well?

Where do you see yourself in Evagrius's description of acedia?

Do you ever use the excuse of being "way too busy" to commit to someone or to something asked of you?

---

[8] Evagrius of Pontus, *Eight Wicked Thoughts,* in *Evagrius Ponticus,* trans. A. M. Casiday, (London: Routledge Books, 2006).

How could you learn to slow down and foster a healthier sense of interiority and calm?

The three "hot" sins begin with avarice, which is our tendency to reduce reality to that which can be counted—whether that enumeration takes place with your bank account, lines on your resume, or even the number of Facebook "friends" you think you enjoy. The result of avarice is an accumulation of stuff along with a loss of self. We forget our true vocation as God's friends as long as our vision and desires are still earthbound:

> There's so much impurity, uncleanness in your heart; love of money constitutes no trifling uncleanness for you. You're hoarding what you can't take away with you. Don't you realize that when you hoard things, you are dragging mud into your heart? So what are you going to see it with, this thing you are seeking? You have filled your safe and shattered your conscience. You're saying to me, "Show me your God." I'm saying to you, "Pay a little attention to your heart." "Show me your God," you say. Attend a little to your heart, I say. Anything you see there, that displeases God, remove it from there. Your God wants to visit you. Listen to the Lord Christ himself: *I and my Father will come to him, and we will take up our abode with him* (Jn 14:23). There you have what God is promising you. So if I promised that I was going to visit your house, you would clean it; God wants to visit your heart, and are you going to be slack about cleaning the house for him? He doesn't enjoy living with love of money, with Avarice, an impure and insatiable woman, whom you were serving, always at her beck and call, while still seeking to see God. What have you done at God's beck and call? What haven't you done at the beck and call of avarice? What have you done at God's beck and call? I'll now show you what's inhabiting your heart, you that want to see God. You see, I said earlier, "There's something to show, but

> there's nobody to show it to." What have you done that God has ordered? What have you put off doing when avarice has ordered it? God ordered you to clothe the naked; you shook in your shoes. Avarice ordered you to strip the clothed bare; you went crazy. If you had done what God ordered, what shall I tell you? You would have this and that? You would have God himself. You did what Avarice ordered, what have you got? I know, you're going to tell me; "I've got what I grabbed." So, you've got by grabbing. You've got something with you, though you've lost yourself?[9]

Always asking his Christian audience to look deeply into their own hearts, Augustine sees the sin of avarice as a major barrier to allowing the Spirit's indwelling. Why do we listen to the material goods around us when God Himself is beckoning? In so doing, we might gain some things but forfeit our own selves.

Gluttony is obviously the sin of overindulgence, usually taking the form of overestimating the need for sensible goods like food and drink. The Fathers never limited gluttony to the corpulent only, knowing that it can also inordinately enrapture the ascetic. Think how the skinny supermodel is just as obsessed and consumed with calories as is the plump gourmand. "Gluttony is hypocrisy of the stomach; for when it is glutted, it complains of scarcity; and when it is loaded and bursting, it cries out that it is hungry."[10]

Lust may be traditionally the least of the deadly sins, but deadly it is. It is understood as reducing another person made in God's image and likeness into a two-dimensional object. In today's image-saturated society, many think lust is inevitable, but with the eyes of the Holy Spirit, one can gaze upon the beauty of another without degrading that person and ruining our own purity in the

---

9 Augustine, *Sermon* 261.5, in *Sermons 230-272B*, trans. Edmund Hill (New Rochelle, NY: New City Press, 1993), 211.

10 John Climacus, *The Ladder of Divine Ascent*, Step 14, "On the clamorous , yet wicked master—the stomach," trans. Archimandrite Lazarus Moore (New York: Harper & Brothers, 1959), 53.

meantime. Until then, unfortunately, the lustful person looks at another only through the strangling lens of his own fallen urges:

> In sensual people (as one who had experienced this passion personally told me after he had got over it) there is a feeling of a sort of love for bodies and a kind of shameless and inhuman spirit which openly asserts itself in the very feeling of the heart. This spirit produces a feeling of physical pain in the heart, fierce as from a blazing stove. As a result of this the sufferer does not fear God, despises the remembrance of punishment as of no consequence, disdains prayer, and during the very act itself regards the body almost as a dead corpse, as though it were an inanimate stone. He is like someone out of his mind and in a trance, perpetually drunk with desire for creatures, rational and irrational. And if the days of this spirit were not cut short, not a soul would be saved, clothed as it is in this clay, mingled with blood and foul moisture. How could they be? For everything created longs insatiably for what is akin to it—blood desires blood, the worm desires a worm, clay desires clay. And does not flesh too desire flesh? Yet we who bridle nature and desire the Kingdom try various tricks to deceive this deceiver. Blessed are they who have not experienced the conflict described above.[11]

Another way of approaching the seven deadly sins is to ask yourself:

What is my major pattern of sin?

What do I know is objectively wrong but tempts me anyway?

---

[11] John Climacus, *The Ladder of Divine Ascent*, Step 15, "On incorruptible purity and chastity to which the corruptible attain by toil and sweat," 58.

What are the hidden thoughts or actions that give me false comfort, even though I know they are not really of God?

See, if you are proud, you can certainly recall moments when you comforted yourself by looking down on others; condescension somehow feels good and makes you feel better about your won lot in life, if even for a second. Everyone is an inconvenience and are rarely your equals.

If you are envious, revenge and secret plotting will sooth your stresses, albeit momentarily. You look for ways to get even, find it hard to be happy at the blessings of others, and are always thinking you have been robbed of what should be yours.

If wrath is your pattern of sin, exploding and lashing out on others will release what you think is ailing you. The littlest annoyance or affront sets you off and you burst out with expletives, slam your fist, and storm off.

If you are slothful, refusing to commit to any one noble thing, constantly repeating the internal litany of "I cannot, I cannot . . ." will justify your acedia. You are paralyzed and have a difficult time being roused to anything important or commit to anything stable.

If avarice and greed have taken over your soul, counting and increasing the numbers of (you fill in the blank) will gladden you. You measure your worth by how much money you have, how many "likes" you have on social media posts, how many lovers you have conquered, and lack any empathy for those who struggle in life.

If you are gluttonous, your mouth appears to be the portal to pleasure. Although you spend hours thinking about food, checking menus, scrolling through websites, you fail to savor your food but eat too eagerly and notice you have to have not only more food but better and finer foods. Perhaps you center your entire lifestyle on staying thin, thinking that any deviation from your perceived "ideal weight" is sinful (remember, Jesus became food!).

If you suffer from lust, reducing others simply to a body pleasing to your own eye, objectifying an eternal person to just two dimensions will slake your cravings, at least for a while. You hide your internet history from those you love, think about others in an inordinately sexual manner, and tend to associate anything sexual with your own personal shame.

What is intriguing in the best of patristic theology is that the Church Fathers refuse to think of the world in an us-versus-them mentality. There are not two kingdoms, only one, however divided amongst itself. All is Christ's, and He has no real competitor. Satan is not evil pure and simple but a rebellious son who valued his own comfort over God's care. In the language of philosophy, existence and goodness are synonymous. If something exists, it is "good"; however, beings with free will who misuse their existence by sinful rebellion are less good than they should be. That said, then, nothing—not even the devil—is pure evil because that would mean pure nothingness. Spiritually speaking, this is why even if we are sinful, our existence gives God glory and why the Church Fathers were rarely stern or severe with the sinful:

> To put the matter briefly, all beings, to the extent that they exist are good and come from the Good and they fall short of goodness and being in proportion to their remoteness from the Good. . . . However, that which is totally bereft of the Good never had, does not have, never shall have, never can have any kind of being at all. Take the example of someone who lives intemperately. He is deprived of the Good in direct proportion to his irrational urges. To this extent he is lacking in being and his desire is for what has no real existence. Nevertheless he has some share in the Good, since there is in him a distorted echo of real love and real unity.[12]

Perhaps God never shuns the sinner and even remains in the evildoer's heart because God knows He can use anything to bring an even greater grace. Anyone can return to the Father, and that is why the Father never leaves us. This is why we begin worship with a Penitential Rite; this is why we "celebrate" the sacrament of Reconciliation; this is why the Gospels are filled with accounts of Jesus being more "at home" with the sinners who know they need a Savior than He is with the religious professionals who look at the law and not at Love.

When we think of how the deadly sins have been categorized, we might recall the parable of the prodigal son.

> Then he said, "A man had two sons, and the younger son said to his father, 'Father, give me the share of your estate that should come to me.' So the father divided the property between them. After a few days, the younger son collected all his belongings and set off to a distant country where he squandered his inheritance on a life of dissipation. When he had freely spent everything, a

---

12 Dionysius the Areopagite, *The Divine Names* IV, 20, in *Psuedo-Dionysius: The Complete Works*, trans. Colm Lubheid (Mahwah, NJ: Paulist Press, 1987), 87.

severe famine struck that country, and he found himself in dire need. So he hired himself out to one of the local citizens who sent him to his farm to tend the swine. And he longed to eat his fill of the pods on which the swine fed, but nobody gave him any. Coming to his senses he thought, 'How many of my father's hired workers have more than enough food to eat, but here am I, dying from hunger. I shall get up and go to my father and I shall say to him, "Father, I have sinned against heaven and against you. I no longer deserve to be called your son; treat me as you would treat one of your hired workers."'

So he got up and went back to his father. While he was still a long way off, his father caught sight of him, and was filled with compassion. He ran to his son, embraced him and kissed him. His son said to him, 'Father, I have sinned against heaven and against you; I no longer deserve to be called your son.' But his father ordered his servants, 'Quickly bring the finest robe and put it on him; put a ring on his finger and sandals on his feet. Take the fattened calf and slaughter it. Then let us celebrate with a feast, because this son of mine was dead, and has come to life again; he was lost, and has been found.' Then the celebration began.

Now the older son had been out in the field and, on his way back, as he neared the house, he heard the sound of music and dancing. He called one of the servants and asked what this might mean. The servant said to him, 'Your brother has returned and your father has slaughtered the fattened calf because he has him back safe and sound.' He became angry, and when he refused to enter the house, his father came out and pleaded with him.

He said to his father in reply, 'Look, all these years I served you and not once did I disobey your orders; yet you never gave me even a young goat to feast on with my friends. But when your son returns who swallowed up your property with prostitutes, for him you slaughter the fattened calf.' He said to him, 'My son, you are here with me always; everything I have is yours. But now we must celebrate and rejoice, because your brother was dead and has come to life again; he was lost and has been found.'" (Lk 15:11–32)

Which son are you? Notice the two ways of disappointing the Father. The younger son sins through the hot sins of avarice, gluttony, and lust. He thinks about nothing other than his own base desires—rejecting his duties (for a while), seeking pleasures in the world, going through all his inheritance in pursuit of tickling his fancies in whatever comes his way.

But is the older son any better? Ironically, he may be even worse. Instead of the flurry of activity down below, the older son stands high looking down on those who return. His heart may not be taken with prostitutes and pleasures, but it is ironically even harder, even colder. The older son easily symbolizes the proud person whose envy and anger are also obvious.

> For some there are who live a perfectly honourable and consistent life, practising every kind of virtuous action, and abstaining from every thing disapproved by the law of God, and crowning themselves with perfect praises in the sight of God and of men: while another is perhaps weak and trodden down, and humbled unto every kind of wickedness, guilty of base deeds, loving impurity, given to covetousness, and stained with all evil. And yet such a one often in old age turns unto God, and asks the forgiveness of his former offences: he prays for mercy, and putting away from him his readiness to fall into sin, sets his affection on virtuous deeds. Or even perhaps when about to close his mortal life, he is admitted to divine baptism, and puts away his offences, God being merciful unto him. And perhaps sometimes persons are indignant at this, and even say, "This man, who has been guilty of such and such actions, and has spoken such and such words, has not paid unto the judge the retribution of his conduct, but has been counted worthy of a grace thus noble and admirable: he has been inscribed among the sons of God, and honoured with the glory of the saints." Such complaints men sometimes give utterance to from an empty narrowness of mind, not conforming to the purpose of the universal Father.[13]

---

13 Cyril of Alexandria, *Homily on Luke* 107, in *A Commentary Upon the Gospel According to S. Luke*, trans. R. Payne Smith (Oxford University Press, 1859), https://www.ccel.org/ccel/pearse/morefathers/files/cyril_on_

The proud do not wait for God to reward their perceived righteousness, but they are depicted as selfishly seizing a crown in order to "crown themselves," as Cyril preaches—outwardly proper but internally demanding praise from both God and man. Like the older son, the proud person is so filled with fear and sternness in keeping the law, there is no room in his heart for rejoicing when the wanderers return to their common Father.

Are you able to identify with anyone in this parable? Are you the younger brother who spent time enamored by the world, lost himself for a time, but came back to the Father? Pray over that return.

Are you the older son who stands assured on his own virtue and tends to look down on sinners and finds it difficult to forgive and rejoice in others' progress in the Spirit? Have you ever been saddened by God's goodness to another, especially an enemy?

Are you the father who has been heartbroken by a loved one and longs to welcome that person home?

Is the "mother" in the house watching out for her children to come home, alerting the Father that in fact one of their sons or daughters is longing to be embraced?

---

luke_10_sermons_99_109.htm#SERMON%20CVII.

The crown the Holy Spirit will in fact give when we finally open our hearts fully to His longing to live within us will replace the crown of thorns we freely wear because of our sins. The flames of Pentecost are depicted as a purifying fire descending upon our minds in order to do just that, to purge them from doubt and despair, from the hot sins which no one else might ever detect but God sees as a barrier and our refusal.

God first used fire to keep us from having to dwell eternally in our sins. For when we were expelled from the Garden of Eden, He stationed a cherubim angel armed with "the fiery revolving sword" in order "to guard the way to the tree of life" (Gn 3:24). God was not going to let us eat from the tree of life, thus staying eternally the way we are (eternalizing sin, in a sense). He now would do everything possible to gain yet again our trust. We see Him going to work all throughout the Old Testament, hitting a crescendo in the incarnation of the Only-Begotten Son. And now as the Holy Spirit descends, God's work in the world realizes both its completion as well as what is needed to extend this new paradise throughout all space and time, the ultimate mission of Christ's Apostolic Church:

> "And there appeared unto them cloven tongues like as of fire, and it sat upon each of them; and they were all filled with the Holy Spirit" (Acts 2:3–4). They partook of fire, not of burning but of saving fire; of fire which consumes the thorns of sins, but gives luster to the soul. This is now coming upon you also, and that to strip away and consume your sins which are like thorns, and to brighten yet more that precious possession of your souls, and to give you grace; for He gave it then to the Apostles. And he sat upon them in the form of fiery tongues, that they might crown themselves with new and spiritual diadems by fiery tongues upon their heads. A fiery sword barred of old the gates of Paradise; a fiery tongue which brought salvation restored the gift.[14]

[14] Cyril of Jerusalem, *Catechetical Lectures,* Lecture 17, no. 15, New Advent translation, https://www.newadvent.org/fathers/310117.htm.

The goal of this retreat is to let the Holy Spirit touch our hearts so as to be transformed into Christians on fire. "A brother came to Abba Arsenius' cell. He half opened the door and saw the Abba as were all on fire."[15]

> While water signifies birth and the fruitfulness of life given in the Holy Spirit, fire symbolizes the transforming energy of the Holy Spirit's actions. The prayer of the prophet Elijah, who "arose like fire" and whose "word burned like a torch," brought down fire from heaven on the sacrifice on Mount Carmel. This event was a "figure" of the fire of the Holy Spirit, who transforms what he touches. John the Baptist, who goes "before [the Lord] in the spirit and power of Elijah," proclaims Christ as the one who "will baptize you with the Holy Spirit and with fire." Jesus will say of the Spirit: "I came to cast fire upon the earth; and would that it were already kindled!" In the form of tongues "as of fire," the Holy Spirit rests on the disciples on the morning of Pentecost and fills them with himself. The spiritual tradition has retained this symbolism of fire as one of the most expressive images of the Holy Spirit's actions. "Do not quench the Spirit." (CCC 696)

> Actually this is why the sacred theologians frequently describe the transcendent and shapeless Being as fiery. . . . Visible fire, after all, is, so to speak, in everything. It passes undiluted through everything and yet continues to be completely beyond them. It lights up everything and remains hidden at the same time. In itself it is undetectable and becomes evident only through its own workings on matter. It is unstoppable. It cannot be looked upon. Yet it is master of everything. Wherever it is, it changes things toward its own activity. It bestows itself upon all who draw near. . . . If ignored it does not seem to be there, but when friction occurs, it will seek out something; it

---

[15] *Sayings of the Desert Fathers,* "Arsenius" §27, in *Roots of Christian Mysticism,* 257. The original collection of these desert sayings began in the late fourth century and gather celebrated aphorisms up through the fifth century, each usually titled after the famous spiritual father or mother known for his or her gift of counsel and ability to turn a phrase.

appears suddenly, naturally and of itself, and soon it rises up irresistibly and, losing nothing of itself, it communes joyfully with everything.[16]

What does fire mean for you? Is it a consoling or a disturbing image?

How might "fire" be needed in your life? Do you need more courage to face problematic situations or to be more honest with those you love?

How would your understanding of "kindness" change upon realizing that the Latin word for "kindness" is *benignity* (we get the word *benign*), literally meaning "good fire" (coming from *bene*—Latin for good or well—and *ignis*—the term for fire)? Have you ever prayed to become "fire," to become aflame with the spirit of love and the freedom to evangelize for Christ to those whom He has put into your life?

---

16 Dionysius the Areopagite, *Celestial Hierarchy*, 15.2, in *Psuedo-Dionysius: The Complete Works*, 184.

When thinking about sin and the Holy Spirit, one verse from Scripture must come to mind, found in each of the synoptic Gospels:

> Therefore, I say to you, every sin and blasphemy will be forgiven people, but blasphemy against the Spirit will not be forgiven. And whoever speaks a word against the Son of Man will be forgiven; but whoever speaks against the holy Spirit will not be forgiven, either in this age or in the age to come. (Mt 12:31–32)

> Amen, I say to you, all sins and all blasphemies that people utter will be forgiven them. But whoever blasphemes against the holy Spirit will never have forgiveness, but is guilty of an everlasting sin. For they had said, "He has an unclean spirit." (Mk 3:28–30)

> Everyone who speaks a word against the Son of Man will be forgiven, but the one who blasphemes against the holy Spirit will not be forgiven. (Lk 12:10)

For centuries, theologians have pondered what exactly the "unforgivable sin" is. One thing is clear: it is against the Holy Spirit. Didymus the Blind begins his treatise on the Holy Spirit strongly warning against this seemingly unforgivable sin: "It is important to investigate all divine matters with reverence and zealous attention, but especially what is said about the divinity of the Holy Spirit, particularly since blasphemy against him is without forgiveness, so much so that the punishment of the blasphemer extends not only throughout the entirety of this present age, but also into the age to come."[17]

With a God who promises to forgive and, like the Good Shepherd, goes out of His way to track down sinners, what could be so blasphemous that it is unpardonable? Saint Athanasius, in his *Against the Arians*, imagines Christ as so humble that He can forgive the sin of denying His divinity, since He comes to us as a man, but there will not be such forgiveness for those who reject the pure godliness of the Holy Spirit:

---

17 Didymus the Blind, *On the Holy Spirit*, trans. Del Cogliano & Ayres (Yonkers: SVS Press, 2011), 143.

> Of course, when he signified that the blasphemy against the Holy Spirit is greater than blasphemy against his humanity, he said, "Whoever would speak a word against the Son of man will have forgiveness" (Mt 12:32). Such were the individuals who said, "Is this not the son of the carpenter?" (Mt 13:55). But they blaspheme against the Holy Spirit and ascribe the words of the Word to the devil. They will have an inevitable punishment. Therefore the Lord, as a man, spoke such things to the Jews, but to the disciples, showing his deity and majesty and signifying that he was not less than the Spirit but equal, he gave them the Spirit and said, "Receive the Holy Spirit" (Jn 20:22) and "I will send him and he will glorify me" (Jn 16:7, 14) and "As many things as he hears, he will speak" (Jn 16:13).[18]

Saint Augustine is of a broader mind, thinking that there is in fact no one particular sin implied here but an overall refusal to think one's sins are actually forgivable.

> But blasphemy against the Spirit, which means opposing this marvelous gift of God with an unrepentant heart until the end of this life, will not be forgiven. . . . After all, God doesn't desire the death of the wicked as much as that they should be converted and live (cf. Ez 33:11), which is why he gave the Holy Spirit to his Church, so that anyone whose sins the Church forgives in the Spirit would be forgiven. But any who persist in hostility to this gift, and instead of asking for it by repentance spurn it by being unrepentant—well, it becomes unforgiveable; not any and every sin, but the actual forgiveness of sins despised or even attacked.[19]

So, for Augustine, it is not one magic moment or not even one particular phrase or curse that is somehow unpardonable, but a life of defiance and unwavering resistance to God's gift of forgiveness up until one's last dying breath. Love will never force itself, regardless

---

18 Athanasius, *Against the Arians* Bk 1.50, in *Trinitarian Controversy*, trans. William Rusch (Philadelphia, Fortress Press, 1980), 114.

19 Augustine of Hippo, *sermon* 71.37, in *Sermons 51-94 on the New Testament*, trans. Edmund Hill (Brooklyn, NY: New City Press, 1991), 269.

how eager it is to gather all in; as such, final impenitence is the only response that is really unforgiveable.

Do you possess what you think is an "unforgivable sin"? Could you finally bring that to the sacrament of Reconciliation?

Do you find it easy to be forgiven or do you continue to condemn yourself even after being properly absolved?

Do you ever presume God's mercy and freely sin, thinking "Oh well, I'll just get to confession on Saturday"?

For the Church Fathers, sin is not so much an action (although it is of course that) but more of an attitude, a coldness and indifference toward a perfect Love offered. God has measured His greatness to our littleness so that we might approach Him without fear or self-doubt. He loves us and therefore comes to us as one of us. In this calibration, God's otherwise unreachable perfections become ours to partake: "For the Father himself loves you, because you have loved me and have come to believe that I came from God" (Jn 16:27). In believing in the inherent holiness of Christ, we too become holy. Let us now leave the first stage of our growth in holiness, purgation from sin, and move on to what it means to be consecrated, to become holy.

Week 5

The Holy Spirit's Indwelling: Consecration

The word *consecration* points to something dedicated to holiness, the sacredness of one who is devoted to God. Holiness is not something added to what it might mean to be human. To be holy is to be fully human. Anything else is ultimately hell. Jesus tells us that we are to become "perfect, just as your heavenly Father is perfect" (Mt 5:48). But in what does perfection consist? Is it intelligence, morality, success, or something more? To be perfect in God's eyes is to be holy, to be "whole" and not divided between Him and all He has made. In short, it is to dwell in God as He dwells in you. Therefore, we shall focus this week on the holiness only the Spirit of God can bring about.

For the fifth week of Easter, the Gospel will be:

> John 14:1–12,
> John 15:1–8, or
> John 13:31–33a, 34–35.

Each of these readings presents Christ as the center of the Easter season, for Christianity is ultimately an encounter with a God who has become man. This Godman is the "way and the truth and the life" (Jn 14:6), the "true vine" (Jn 15:1), and the Master who paradoxically is also "the Son of Man" glorified through rejection and crucifixion (Jn 13:31). In each of these Gospels, Christ uses His own life to point us to the Father. As we near His ascension, the Son is assuring us that He has brought us into His own holiness, partakers of the "divine nature" (2 Pt 1:4), and that in our accepting the Son, we have also received the Father.

> No man therefore will come to the Father, that is, will appear as a partaker of the Divine nature, save through Christ alone. For if He had not become a Mediator by taking human form, our condition could never have advanced to such a height of blessedness; but now, if any one approach the Father in a spirit of faith and reverent knowledge, he will do so, by the help of our Saviour Christ Himself. For even as I said just now, so I will say again, the course of the argument being in no wise different. By accepting the Son truly as Son a man will arrive also at the knowledge of God the Father: for one could not be looked upon as a son, except the father who begat him were fully acknowledged at the same time. The knowledge of the Father is thus necessarily concurrent with belief in the Son, and knowledge of the Son with belief in the Father. And so the Lord says most truly: No man cometh unto the Father but by Me. For the Son is in nature and essence an Image of God the Father, and not (as some have thought) a Being moulded merely into His likeness by attributes specially bestowed, Himself being by nature something essentially different, and being so esteemed.[1]

For most of us, holiness is a very abstract concept, a flight of fancy that seems reserved for the monk or consecrated nun. It is a state of life far, far away from the stresses of my life, something very distant from my financial pressures, commute to work, or the day-to-day anxieties of marriage and raising children. Not long ago when the foundress of the Catholic Worker Movement,

---

1 Cyril of Alexandria, *Commentary on John 14*, "Patristic Bible Commentary," https://sites.google.com/site/aquinasstudybible/home/gospel-of-john-commentary/cyril-on-john-13/cyril-on-john-14.

Dorothy Day (now being considered for canonization by the Catholic Church), was listed as one of *Time* magazine's "living saints," she fired back, "That's the way people try to dismiss you. If you're a saint, then you must be impractical and utopian, and nobody has to pay any attention to you. That kind of talk makes me sick." Tough words from a tough woman, and maybe soon from a tough saint. Day did not want to be easily dismissed as a saint, knowing if she were, her insistence that the hungry be fed and the homeless be housed would be pushed aside as the exclusive work of professional religious and not a call for everyone.

If holiness seems too distant, too difficult, ponder Cyril's words above: you will advance in godliness "by the help of our Saviour Christ Himself." Among the earliest heresies the Church had to face is one associated with the British monk Pelagius (d. 418) who hobnobbed with the rich and famous in Rome and fled on their ships in 410 when the Visigoths invaded Rome. Landing on the shores of Northern Africa, this strong-headed monk met the "Doctor of Grace," Saint Augustine of Hippo (d. 430). The clash between these two minds was fierce, and their impact has lasted through the centuries. On the one hand, Pelagius argued that salvation was in our hands and if we worked hard enough, we would come to merit all that God longs to give us. On the other side, Bishop Augustine insisted that we are all children of Adam and any good we do requires God's grace and without grace we can move only further and further away from God. The solution, Augustine counseled, is to quit trying to secure divine favor, rest in the Lord, and open one's heart up to whatever God chooses to give.

In short, Pelagius's heresy (repeated by so many other rigorist groups) was that there is good in us that God did not put there, and in order to win God's favor, we work harder and lift our achievements up to Him. Augustine, however, knew from his own experience the habituating power of sin, and he read Saint Paul who said that all the good in us is divine favor and that our salvation has more to do with our "ceasing" than our acting—that is, we cease resisting that eternal invitation to draw close to Christ, to fall on our knees and embrace the Crucified One.

Augustine did in fact throw himself to the ground and wept copious tears when the Lord drew near. Here was a man who knew he was not strong enough to live a holy life, and so he made receptivity and humility the characteristics of Catholic power. We are not the agents of our salvation; we are the bride, we are the beneficiary, the son or the daughter.

Is your Christian life something you realize is a total gift? Do you think of your virtue and spiritual successes as ways God loves you more or as manifestations of God's love for you?

Do you find it easier to give or to receive a gift? How might this affect your understanding of grace, of God's gifts to you?

How do you try to win or merit God's love? Do you make "quid pro quo" or "deal" prayers with Him?

How might you grow in humility—that is, in a totally honest estimation of all that you are and have, realized as God's laboring in and through you?

Without bodies, angels need not worry about time or space. But we do. Have you ever considered the best place, best time, best bodily posture and frame of mind in which to pray? In becoming human, God has now shown He wants to meet us as we are, where we are, how we are. This gives us insight into how we should understand holiness as well. Our consecration will not be something apart from the life we are now living. God does not expect us to think of the lives He has given us as distractions or as challenges to the holiness He wants to bring about in us. Your family, your career, your passions and pastimes are all able to effect greater sanctity to the Lord when united to His holy will.

We therefore approach the Spirit's desire to consecrate our lives by first examining the role of our corporeality, our embodiment, and all that might mean for our growth in sanctity. This was not something lost on the first Christians:

> For all the favors we enjoy we bless the Creator of all, through his Son Jesus Christ and through the Holy Spirit. On the day which is called Sunday we have a common assembly of all who live in the cities or in the outlying districts, and the memoirs of the Apostles or the writings of the Prophets are read, as long as there is time. . . . Then we all stand up together and offer up our prayers. . . . Sunday, indeed, is the day on which we all hold our common assembly because it is the first day on which God, transforming the darkness and matter, created the world, and our Savior Jesus Christ rose from the dead on the same day.[2]

> If you are at home pray at the third hour [nine o'clock] and praise God. If you are elsewhere at that moment praise God in your heart, for at that hour Christ was nailed to the Cross. . . . You will pray likewise at the sixth hour [midday] remembering Christ hanging on the cross while . . . the darkness reigned. At

2 Justin Martyr, *First Apology* 67, in *The First Apology, The Second Apology, Dialogue with Trypho, Exhortation to the Greeks, Discourse to the Greeks, The Monarchy of the Rule of God*, trans. Thomas Falls (Washington, DC: Catholic University of America Press [1948] 2008), 1067.

that hour you will offer a very fervent prayer to imitate him who prayed for his executioners when the universe was plunged in darkness. At the ninth hour [three o'clock in the afternoon] resume your prayer and praise. . . . At that hour Christ, his side pierced, poured out water and blood. He illumined the declining daylight until evening and offered a symbol of the resurrection with the return of the light.

Pray also before your body goes to sleep. Towards the middle of the night get up, wash your hands in water, and pray. If your wife is there, pray together. If she is not yet a Christian, withdraw into another room to pray, then go back to bed. Do not be negligent over your prayer. One who is married is in no way defiled. "He who has bathed does not need to wash . . . but he is clean all over" (Jn 13:10). If you make the sign of the cross with your moist breath your body will be clean all over, right down to your feet. For the gift of the Spirit and the water of baptism, flowing as from a spring, have cleansed the believer, if he has received them with a heart full of faith.[3]

We all pray facing East, but few realize that we do this because we are seeking paradise, our old fatherland, which God planted in the East in Eden. We all stand for prayer on Sunday, but not everyone knows why. We stand for prayer on the day of the Resurrection to remind our selves of the grace we have been given: not only because we have been raised with Christ and are obliged to seek the things that are above, but also because Sunday seems to be an image of the age to come. Notice that although Sunday is the beginning of the days, Moses does not call it the first day, but one day: "And there was evening and there was morning, one day" (Gen 1:5). . . . This day foreshadows the state which is to follow the present age: a day without sunset, nightfall, or successor, an age which does not grow old or come to an end. It is necessary for the Church to teach her newborn children to stand for prayer on this day, so that they will always be reminded of eternal life, and not neglect preparations for the journey. The entire season of

---

3 *Apostolic Tradition* §35, in *Roots of Christian Mysticism*, trans. Olivier Clément (Hyde Park, NY: New City Press, 1995), 192–93.

> Pentecost is likewise a reminder of the resurrection we expect in the age to come.[4]

Those who live consecrated by the Spirit see everyday realities as microcosms of the great Christian mysteries: Sunday is the day of both the creation of the universe (an ancient Patristic belief) as well as, more importantly, the recreation of God's Kingdom. The hours of each day commemorate the passion and death of the Crucified Lord, creating a certain "muscle memory" in His followers throughout the day that the morning sunrise is a mark of the Resurrection, the early afternoon hours recall His road to Calvary, and the evening symbolizes the eternal rest of peace that awaits God's chosen.

> We bless thee now, O my Christ, thou Word of God,
> Light of Light without beginning, Bestower of the Spirit.
> We bless thee, threefold light of undivided glory.
> Thou hast vanquished the darkness and brought forth the light,
> to create everything in it.
>
> Thou hast given solidity to matter,
> moulding the face of the world
> and the shape of its beauty therein.
> Thou hast enlightened the human spirit,
> endowing it with reasoning and wisdom.
> Everywhere is to be found the reflection of eternal light,
> so that in the light the human spirit
> may find its splendour and become entirely light.
>
> Thou hast illumined the sky with spangled lights.
> The night and the day thou hast commanded to alternate in peace
> by giving them, for rule, brotherly love.
> Night puts an end to the body's toil,
> Day awakens us again to our work, to our business that engrosses us.
> But we are fleeing the darkness,

---

4 Basil of Caesarea, *On the Holy Spirit* 27.66, trans. David Anderson (Crestwood, NY: St. Vladimir's Seminary Press, 1980), 100–1.

we are hastening to the day that never wanes,
to the day that will never know the sorrow of the dusk.

Grant to mine eyelids a light sleep,
that my voice remain not long dumb.
Thy creation shall keep watch to sing psalms with the angels.
May my sleep be ever peopled by thy presence . . .
Even parted from the body my spirit sings thy praise
O Father, Son and Holy Spirit.
To thee be glory and power
for ever and ever. Amen.[5]

There is no moment, no passing, nothing too insignificant that cannot somehow speak to us of a God who not only created all of these realities but took them on personally as well. In Jesus Christ, the Creator also experienced sunrises and sunsets, He too practiced different bodily postures while praying with His Father—standing, kneeling, sitting in the Synagogue—and He too knew what it was like to anticipate the coming of seasons and festivals. In Him, nothing human is opposed to the divine.

Because this world is dripping with the divine presence, the Fathers saw holiness even in sub-human creation. In fact, according to Tertullian, every creature prays simply by being what it was created to be: "Indeed, every angel prays, every creature. The herds and the wild beasts pray and bend their knees, coming forth from byres and dens looking to heaven, giving movement to the spirit after their fashion with animated mouths. And even now the birds arise, lifting themselves to heaven, spreading out their wings like a cross whilst uttering what appears to be a prayer. What more might be said on the duty of prayer? Even the Lord himself prayed, and to him be honor and might forever and ever."[6]

---

5 Gregory Nazianzus, "Evening Hymn," in *Dogmatic Poems, Roots of Christian Mysticism*, 193–94.

6 Tertullian, *On Prayer*, §29 in *Tertullian, Cyprian, Origen On the Lord's Prayer*, trans. Alistair Stewart-Sykes (Crestwood, NY: St. Vladimir's Press, 2004), 64.

Have we grown so techno-centered that we have lost our connection to God's presence throughout all of creation? Or have we grown so suspicious of anyone who cares about nature that we dismiss anything "green" as propaganda? But if we listen to the Church Fathers' praising God through the intricacies and beauties of the natural realm, we might renew a sense of awe and gratitude.

> But now ask the beasts to teach you, the birds of the air to tell you; Or speak to the earth to instruct you, and the fish of the sea to inform you. Which of all these does not know that the hand of God has done this? In his hand is the soul of every living thing, and the life breath of all mortal flesh. (Job 12:7–10)

> Bless the Lord, all you works of the Lord. . . . All you waters above the heavens . . . sun and moon . . . stars of heaven . . .fire and heat . . . hoarfrost and snow . . . nights and days . . . light and darkness, bless the Lord. (Dn 3:52–81)

Throughout the Christian Tradition, we see how all creation praises its Creator. The lower beings glorify God by fulfilling their "vocation" to be what they were created to be, and God looks lovingly down on all that is "very good." Only angels and humans, those beings created with free will, can disappoint the Lord by consciously turning away from our vocations to fulfill our ends as saints. That is why every cell of our existence, all our experiences and day-to-day realities, must be consecrated, and that is what creation screams for us to do.

Do you keep the Sabbath? How in particular do you honor the Lord's day?

Do you have any habit of a particular prayer in or for the morning, one at midday, or at 3 p.m., and then again in the evening hours?

Do you ever ask the Lord or Our Lady what they are praying for and how you can assist them in this intercession for the world?

Does nature speak to you of God's authorship? Where in creation do you most readily find God?

One area of consecration the Church Fathers concentrated on was the use of our bodies. Brute animals don't have souls that can consciously praise the Lord, and angels do not have bodies with which to do it. But we do, and that makes us the most unique creatures alive: bridges between heaven and earth, frontier creatures who belong in both heaven and earth. That is why we do not pray with just our minds but with all we are.

Tertullian coined a memorable phrase when he summed the Christian Faith up in these three words: *caro cardo salutis*, "the flesh is the hinge of salvation."[7] The greatest scandal Jesus wrought was the fact that God saves us as one of us, an embodied human with passions and emotions, with hair and fingernails and all the limitations and exultations that come from being embodied. In the Incarnation, God was no longer just everywhere, He was now *somewhere*, and that is why space and time have been consecrated, allowing Christians to talk about a "sacred space" or a "holy time."

Of course, literally speaking, for the Christian, all space and all time is just as "holy" as any other; what makes a place holy is the presence of the incarnate Lord. Think, for example, how Catholics do not genuflect on Good Friday or Holy Saturday when the tabernacle sits empty. It is Christ, our Most Sacred Host, that transforms

---

7 Tertullian, *On the Resurrection of the Flesh* §8, our translation.

that space into an encounter with the Holy of Holies, not the wood or gold or linens, however beautiful they may be. It is the same with time: the liturgical seasons heighten our senses and raise our minds to a new time (e.g., Advent or Lent, Christmas or the Easter Octaves). "The Most High does not dwell in houses made by human hands" (Acts 7:48; cf. Acts 17:24), but we do and that is why paying attention to how we pray with our hands and bodies is important, and why we consecrate seasons and days to remind us that our God is always and ever at work in our world.

I have stretched out my hands in offering to the Lord.
The hands stretched out are a sign thereof,
upright with hands stretched out,
the wood of the cross set up.
Alleluia![8]

Among the more scandalous things Saint Paul told his Jewish brothers and sisters was that the old temple had been relocated from a fixed point only in Jerusalem to the bodies of the baptized. While the morality and the modesty of the people of Paul's time would put twenty-first century America to great shame, Paul seeks to instruct them that they should realize that they conduct themselves properly because the Holy Spirit has claimed each of us as the place where He now indwells: "Do you not know that your body is a temple of the Holy Spirit within you, whom you have from God, and that you are not your own? For you have been purchased at a price. Therefore, glorify God in your body" (1 Cor 6:19–20). That is, our bodies are only "on loan." We are not the landlords but the tenants of all we are and have: "None of us lives for oneself, and no one dies for oneself. For if we live, we live for the Lord, and if we die, we die for the Lord; so then, whether we live or die, we are the Lord's. For this is why Christ died and came to life, that he might be Lord of both the dead and the living" (Rom 14:7–9).

---

8 Odes of Solomon §27, in *Roots of Christian Mysticism*, 197.

Through the sin of entitlement—a modern manifestation of the old sin of pride—we can slowly come to believe that we are the masters of our bodies, our gender (or "identity"), and even our souls. We possess the God-given ability to do with these things as we might see fit; in that sense, free will is a double-edged gift. God allows us to have our needs met, on our own terms at our own peril, but He does all He possibly can to have us choose our joy on His terms. The battered Body and Blood of Jesus Christ is the evidence He provides, manifestations of a love that has ransomed us from the harlotry of a world where bodies and persons are cheap and disposable:

> But he has spoken of these things as God's, not only because he brought them into being, but also because, when they were alienated, he won them again a second time, paying as the price, the blood of the Son. Mark how he brought the whole to completion in Christ, how he raised us up into heaven. You are members of Christ, says he, you are a temple of the Spirit. Become not then members of a harlot: for it is not your body which is insulted; since it is not your body at all, but Christ's. And these things he spoke, both to make manifest his loving-kindness in that our body is his, and to withdraw us from all evil license. For if the body be another's, you have no authority, says he, to insult another's body; and especially when it is the Lord's; nor yet to pollute a temple of the Spirit. For if anyone who invades a private house and makes his way revelling into it, must answer for it most severely; think what dreadful things he shall endure who makes a temple of the King a robber's lurking place.[9]

The human body is immersed into the Holy Spirit at Baptism. This consecration was so powerful and real, some of the Church Fathers argued that the Spirit never leaves the flesh, even after one's death. This gave rise to the veneration of relics, pilgrimages to the tombs of the saints, and so on. Jesus started it, locating God in

---

9 John Chrysostom *Homilies on First Corinthians* 18.3 (on 1 Cor 6:15-20), New Advent translation, https://www.newadvent.org/fathers/220118.htm.

human flesh and bones, and the saints continue it, even after their souls ascend into heaven:

> Before baptism, one is called the old person, but after baptism the new person (cf. Eph 4:22–24). Now the Holy Spirit is the abiding Soul of the new person and he remains, not only during the body's life, but also after its death, and in the case of the saints he performs miracles and works signs. For the bones of the just, that is to say, of the apostles and martyrs and all the saints, while they do not have any natural soul left in them—for that left them at their death—still have the Holy Spirit abiding with them, and it is he who effects signs and wonders in them; and demonic spirits cry out bitterly at his power within them, for sicknesses are driven off and illnesses chased away.[10]

It was not that long ago that an altar consecrated before the Second Vatican Council had to contain a relic of a saint, a visible extension of the Spirit of holiness the Word-Made-Flesh pours into those who approach Him.

Are you in the practice of using sacramentals? That is, do you have good religious art and items in your home and readily available to use for prayer? Do you carry a rosary into your everyday life?

Do you ever practice with different prayer positions? Kneeling, standing, sitting, hands raised high, hands folded, and so on?

---

[10] Mar Philoxenus of Mabbug, *On the Indwelling of the Holy Spirit*; trans. Sebastian Brock (Kalamazoo, MI: Cistercian Publications, 1987), 122–23.

Do you have icons in your home? Think about preparing a place used just for prayer—a corner in your home or a place that you could decorate with reminders of God and the saints' presence.

Have you ever entertained making a pilgrimage somewhere?

This brief look at the consecrated body should make it clear that Christians look at the human person differently than the rest of the world. Philosophers opposed to Christian wisdom have reduced the human to either a soul clumsily inhabiting a body for a while (this is the popular philosophy of the Enlightenment, famously caricaturizing the soul as a "ghost in a machine") or as a mere collection of electric synapses and hormonal urges (the reigning philosophy of modernity). For the Christian, however, the human person is an embodied spirit, a spiritualized body, one who is naturally and eternally both body and soul. Our loved ones who die do not become angels, nor should we ever think that we are just our bodies or our minds. We are created composite beings, and we shall be raised and beatified as both body and soul, and that is precisely why God took on a body, to unite and redeem all we are.

But of course the body and all that being embodied means—space and time, emotions and dreams, anxieties and stresses—is nothing without the soul. The body is good and the flesh is exactly how the Son of God seeks to save each and every one of us. So when Christians talk about the "battle against the flesh," it is not the body that is the enemy but the "fleshy" way our fallen minds can tend to go.

> For those who live according to the flesh are concerned with the things of the flesh, but those who live according to the

> spirit with the things of the spirit. The concern of the flesh is death, but the concern of the spirit is life and peace. For the concern of the flesh is hostility toward God; it does not submit to the law of God, nor can it; and those who are in the flesh cannot please God. But you are not in the flesh; on the contrary, you are in the spirit, if only the Spirit of God dwells in you. Whoever does not have the Spirit of Christ does not belong to him. (Rom 8:5–9)

To consecrate "the flesh," we must consecrate the soul, our minds. We must learn that what keeps us from God is never our bodies but our conscious decision to keep God away, to live our lives on our terms and not His. The decision is daily, the decision is ours, and that is why it is paramount that we allow our thoughts and passions, our emotions and images, be consecrated by the Holy Spirit.

> Brother, nothing is to be gained by consulting your spiritual father about all the thoughts that come into your mind. Most of them quickly disappear. You need to ask about those that persist and make war on you. . . .
>
> Brother, do not try yourself to discern the thoughts that come into your mind. You are not capable. . . . If they worry you . . . cast your powerlessness before God, saying, "Lord, I am in thy hands, come to my help." . . . As for the thought that persists in you and makes war on you, tell it to your Abba and by God's grace he will cure you.[11]

If you struggle with your racing thoughts, learn from this sixth-century spiritual master from the Egyptian desert: you cannot control what thoughts come in and out of your head, but you can learn to control those fixations and ideations that bring only stress and frustration. The first step in healing here is realizing that your mind is not an isolated silo but can be the place where the Holy Spirit meets you. In this sense, no one is ever really alone. The Spirit hovers over each of our intellects as He did those first Apostles at Pentecost.

---

11 Barsanuphius, *Letters* 165 and 142 respectively, in *Roots of Christian Mysticism*, 148.

Barsanuphius recommends an ancient practice in Christian spirituality: to bring your tormenting thoughts to a trusted friend. This might be your best friend or your local confessor, but the key is to realize that the enemy of our human nature wants us to isolate ourselves and allow only him into our consciousness. Satan hates the light; he runs when we are trusting and transparent with our innermost thoughts. Hiding our truest selves is a sign of shame, as Adam and Eve began to hide in the Garden after their sin. The Holy Spirit will never force Himself into our psyches, for He created them free, but He will wait, often nudging us in His way so we might finally let Him in.

Many of the Church Fathers drew from the stories of liberation found in the Bible to describe this surrender of our minds to the Holy Spirit. Maximus the Confessor likens our consecration to our leaving the slavery of Egypt and making our way to the Promised Land where we can finally be free from tormenting thoughts and habitual sin. To make this exodus, we must trust that God desires this intimacy and that all that God has revealed for our salvation is already inscribed into the heart that desires to know Him:

> And to put it concisely, one who does not place himself under the yoke of sin, nor allow himself to be suffocated by the foul torrent of the passions through evil desire and lifted up by sense to enjoy the fountain of pleasures, but rather puts to death the way of thinking that belongs to the flesh, which tyrannizes over the soul's nobility, and is raised above everything that is subject to corruption and flees this erring world like a kind of Egypt . . . he becomes unutterably conversant with God, as in a cloud and unknowing, and is inscribed by the finger of God, the Holy Spirit, within himself, within his mind, with the dogmas of piety, and outside, like Moses and the tablets, with the graces of virtue.[12]

---

12 Maximus the Confessor, *Difficulties* 10.22b, in *Maximus the Confessor*, trans. Andrew Louth (New York: Routledge Early Church Fathers Series, 1996), 122.

While Maximus compared our growth in holiness to an adventure *without,* Origen had earlier compared it to a journey *within.* He compares our new life in the Spirit not as something we deserve from the outside but something we discover already present inside the sanctified soul through God's incessant grace. God has always been at work in you, but now He is asking you to be more intentional, more conscious, in sweeping away all that is not of Him and finding the essence of who you think you are as His beloved son or daughter:

> For he is present there, the Word of God, and his work is to remove the earth from the soul of each one of you, to let your spring flow freely. This spring is in you and does not come from outside because "the kingdom of God is in the midst of you" (Lk 17:21). It was not outside but in her house that the woman who had lost her silver coin found it again (Lk 15:8). She had lighted the lamp and swept out the house, and it was there that she found her silver coin. For your part, if you light your "lamp", if you make use of the illumination of the Holy Spirit, if you "see light in his light", you will find the silver coin in you. For the image of the heavenly king is in you. When God made human beings at the beginning he made them "in his own image and likeness" (Gen 1:26). And he does not imprint this image on the outside but within them. It could not be seen in you as long as your house was dirty, full of refuse and rubbish . . . but, rid by the Word of God of that great pile of earth that was weighing you down, let the "image of the heavenly" shine out in you now. . . . The maker of this image is the Son of God. He is a craftsman of such surpassing skill that his image may indeed be obscured by neglect, but never destroyed by evil. The image of God remains in you always.[13]

Gregory of Nyssa likewise insisted that our surrender to the Holy Spirit is not something foreign to being human, but rather it is precisely for this encounter that humanity was created. Revealed as a dove, the Spirit of God rests in what is His own, clearing out the filth which we foolishly took on as something we thought would bring

---

13 Origen, *Homilies on Genesis* 1.4, in *Roots of Christian Mysticism,* 131.

happiness. Like the Son in the womb of Mary, the Spirit descends into His Church in order to raise us on His wings to the Father. In so doing, the Spirit elevates our human nature to things divine:

> But how can anyone reach to this, whose ambitions creep below? How can anyone fly up into the heavens, who has not the wings of heaven and is not already buoyant and lofty-minded by reason of a heavenly calling? Few can be such strangers to evangelic mysteries as not to know that there is but one vehicle on which man's soul can mount into the heavens, viz. the self-made likeness in himself to the descending Dove, whose wings David the Prophet also longed for. This is the allegorical name used in Scripture for the power of the Holy Spirit; whether it be because not a drop of gall is found in that bird, or because it cannot bear any noisome smell, as close observers tell us. He therefore who keeps away from all bitterness and all the noisome effluvia of the flesh, and raises himself on the aforesaid wings above all low earthly ambitions, or, more than that, above the whole universe itself, will be the man to find that which is alone worth loving, and to become himself as beautiful as the Beauty which he has touched and entered.[14]

> When your mind in great yearning for God as it were withdraws by degrees from the flesh and, being filled with piety and joy, deflects all representations from perception, memory or temperament, then reckon that you have come near to the boundaries of prayer.[15]

Do you trust that God has chosen you as a friend and longs to speak with you?

---

[14] Gregory of Nyssa, *On Virginity* §11, New Advent translation, https://www.newadvent.org/fathers/2907.htm.

[15] Evagrius of Pontus, *On Prayer* §62, in *Evagrius Ponticus*, trans. A. M. Casiday, (London: Routledge Books, 2006), 192.

How do you discern God's voice from your own, or even the voices of the world?

Do you struggle with ruminating on various hurts or holding grudges? Do you fixate on a particular point of doctrine or politics? What might the Holy Spirit want to do with these thoughts?

What do you allow into your mind that you know is causing psychic harm, changing you into someone you do not want to be? Is it images from the internet; is it the divisions in our world, in our Church? How can you let the Holy Spirit combat this for you? "Finally, brothers, whatever is true, whatever is honorable, whatever is just, whatever is pure, whatever is lovely, whatever is gracious, if there is any excellence and if there is anything worthy of praise, think about these things" (Phil 4:8).

Can you try to foster a constant mentality of gratitude? Going through your day thanking God for all the ways He watches over you, blesses you, and loves you—being grateful for your getting out of bed, for the people in your life, for the life you are leading, and so on—is the only way to understand the depths of God and to have your own divided heart mended as well.

The Holy Spirit is united eternally and equally to the Word. Our breath and our mind should therefore be one as well. When we live that concretely in the Holy Spirit, our lives begin to change and our life with Christ is no longer just a religious or Sunday affair; it becomes our very lifeline, our every breath. When Saint Antony of the Desert was dying, he called in his closest companions and told them that they must preserve the holiness infused in them by the Spirit by "breathing Christ" and making Him their very life:

> He said to them, "I, as it is written go the way of the fathers" (Josh 23:14), for I perceive that I am called by the Lord. And do you be watchful and destroy not your long discipline, but as though now making a beginning, zealously preserve your determination. For you know the treachery of the demons, how fierce they are, but how little power they have. Wherefore fear them not, but rather ever breathe Christ, and trust him. Live as though dying daily. Give heed to yourselves, and remember the admonition you have heard from me. Have no fellowship with the schismatics, nor any dealings at all with the heretical Arians. For you know how I shunned them on account of their hostility to Christ, and the strange doctrines of their heresy. Therefore be the more earnest always to be followers first of God and then of the Saints; that after death they also may receive you as well-known friends into the eternal habitations.[16]

How we choose to spend this life will determine how God lets us choose to spend the next: if we strive for union with Him now, we shall enjoy it forever; if we feed the hungry here, we shall be invited to the eternal banquet of heaven; if we refute the heretic and admonish the sinner, we shall be gathered into the eternal Church of Christ's saintly friends.

One piece of counsel Antony the Great leaves us here is to recognize the "little power" of the demons. Our fallen passions and the temptations that come to us from the outside have little power over us. At this point in the retreat, we can easily recognize and

---

16 St. Athanasius, *Life of Antony* §91, New Advent translation, https://www.newadvent.org/fathers/2811.htm.

acknowledge our obvious sins, and that is why we need to consecrate our wills and our minds to the Spirit of Truth and Goodness. But a more subtle tactic of the devil is to get us to weigh our worthiness before the Father in terms of the good we have done and the evil we have avoided.

It is right that we strive to root out sin in our lives; that is a given. What is not so clear always is how the Law no longer saves us; only love saves us. This is the point of Pentecost: we have been made temples of the Holy Spirit, and God's commandments are now not just a code of ethics etched on stone but deep impressions onto our hearts, where He now dwells. As we grow in holiness, we can all too often slip into the snare of tallying our virtues and our vices, and so try to impress God and win over His care for us.

> The hearts of all Catholics know well, dearly beloved, that today's solemnity ought to be honored among the special feasts. No one doubts how much reverence is owed to this day which the Holy Spirit has consecrated by the wonderful miracle of his own gift. For, from that day on which the Lord ascended over all the heights of heaven to sit at the right hand of God the Father, this day is the tenth. It is likewise the fiftieth from the Resurrection of that same Lord who enlightened us about him from whom light began. It contains great mysteries in itself of both the old and the new dispensations, by which it is very clearly shown that the grace was foretold by the old law and that the law was fulfilled by grace. As once to the Hebrew people, freed from Egypt, the law was given on Mount Sinai on the fiftieth day from his Resurrection, the Holy Spirit came down on the Apostles and the community of believers. The attentive Christian can easily know that the beginnings of the Old Testament had ministered to the principles of the Gospel, and that the Second Covenant was established by the same Spirit who had set up the first.[17]

---

17 Leo the Great, *Sermon* 75.1, in *St. Leo the Great: The Sermons,* trans. Jane Freeland and Agnes Conway (Washington, DC: Catholic University of America Press, 2996), 330–31.

Week 6

The Holy Spirit Brings Us to Jesus: Communion

The sixth week of Easter brings us into the "farewell discourse" of Jesus before He ascends to the Father. Gratefully, He spends a great amount of time assuring us that He is not really leaving us, for He has established His Most Blessed Sacrament as the means by which He continues to be literally and physically present. Additionally, He promises us a new Spirit, the Holy Spirit, who will come and comfort us and teach us all things.

This week's Gospel proclamations will therefore be:

John 14:15–21,
John 15:9–17, or
John 14:23–29.

These Gospels all promise us that the bond now created between Christ and Christian is so strong that it cannot be undone. We are the many branches grafted onto the one life-giving Vine. We are those in whom the Son now lives, redeeming us and saving us from lives of loneliness and desolation: "I will not leave you orphans; I will come to you. In a little while the world will no longer see me, but you will see me, because I live and you will live. On that day you will realize that I am in my Father and you are in me and I in you. Whoever has my commandments and observes them is the one who loves me. And whoever loves me will be loved by my Father, and I will love him and reveal myself to him" (Jn 14:18–21).

We also celebrate the Ascension this week. While it has traditionally been on that first Thursday (making the original nine-day novena possible), today many Catholic dioceses have transferred Ascension Thursday to the sixth Sunday, rendering those readings:

> Matthew 28:16–20 (A),
> Mark 16:15–20 (B), or
> Luke 24:46–53 (C).

We can celebrate Christ's bodily ascension into heaven only because He has first promised never to "leave us orphans." By instituting His Eucharist, Christ does indeed remain with us. But He remains with us in a way that "the world no longer sees" Him, but "we do see Him" because we have the eyes of the Spirit, deified eyes that not only perceive the superficial appearances of things but enable us to pierce to the heart of reality. While the world may see only bread and wine, we behold the Body and Blood of Christ. It is this Lord who comes to us, dwells within us, and makes us like Himself.

This is the heart of communion: the transformative power of love. In the words of the Church Fathers, this is the entire and only goal of Christianity. Or as Saint Athanasius summed up the entire Christian faith by explaining how the Son of God "indeed, assumed humanity that we might become God."[1] This can strike our ears as an alarming statement, but it is the heart of all the Church Fathers' theology and pastoral work, and we shall spend this next week unpacking what this means and how to understand it in a totally and faithfully orthodox manner.

In one way, this entire week's readings from the Fathers have to do with something that is already in us, something we have all both experienced and long for more of: love. While God is certainly

---

1 *On the Incarnation* §54, in *St. Athanasius on the Incarnation*, trans. A Religious of C.S.M.V. (Crestwood, NY: St. Vladimir Seminary Press, [1944] 1989), 93.

"loving" in the Old Testament, and while Islam has ninety-nine official names for God, "Love" is not among them. This is not to make the pretentious claim that the God of Judaism or of Islam is not loving—that is for Jews and Muslims to decide—but it is to admit that "God is love" is found only in the Christian Scriptures: "Whoever is without love does not know God, for God is love" (1 Jn 4:8).

So why are Christians unique in proclaiming God as pure charity? Because it requires a Trinity to experience love, or as Saint Augustine so succinctly put it, "Oh but you do see a trinity if you see charity."[2] That is: wherever love occurs, there is always a lover, a beloved, and the love that unites them. Christians alone understand God as love because only Christians know that the heart of God's essence is a loving Father, His Beloved Son, and the Holy Spirit who is the Love uniting these two "before all ages."

Transformative union is the characteristic of love. Love is more than a side-by-side connection (and that is why a personal relationship with Jesus is good but never enough); love is when one begins to live as the other—when his or her joys and sorrows become mine. It is to realize that you have become the other, that your heart beats in the heart of that other, and that you two now live in a bond that "is patient, is kind, is not jealous, is not pompous, not inflated, not rude, it does not seek its own interests, it is not quick-tempered, it does not brood over injury, it does not rejoice over wrongdoing but rejoices with the truth. It bears all things, believes all things, hopes all things, endures all things" (1 Cor 13:4–7).

How do you define *love*? It is one of those words where we know what we mean until someone asks us. In traditional Christianity, love is defined by two things: benevolence and union. That is, we both wish the best possible life for the other and work to make that happen, and second, we long to be in the actual presence of that person forever. That is love, and that is exactly why God came to earth. He came to give us the most possible life—heavenly bliss—and He came as one of us so as to be with us for all time. If there is

---

2 Augustine, *On the Trinity* 8.8.12, in *The Trinity*, trans. Edmund Hill (Hyde Park, NY: New City Press, 2012), 253.

someone in your life you say you "love" but sin against or with that person, that is not love; if there is someone you say you "love" but do not want to be in heaven with, that is not love.

Another primal sign of love is bringing something into existence. When a husband and a wife love each other, they long for another to love.

> God is the producer and generator of tenderness and eros. He has set outside himself what was within himself, namely, creatures. Which is why it is said of him: God is Love. The Song of Songs calls him agape, or "sensual pleasure," and "desire," which means eros. In so far as the eros desire originates from him, he can be said to be the moving force of it, since he generated it. But in so far as he is himself the true object of the love, he is the moving force in others who look to him and possess according to their own nature the capacity for desire.[3]

Hopefully by now you are seeing that Christianity is really the map of the human heart. It is what we all desire: to be known perfectly, to be loved perfectly, to be infinitely forgiven, and to have a love that is never selfishly exclusive but can encompass all whom we hold dear. In assuming the fullness of humanity to Himself, the New Adam alone makes this possible—to have a love that unites us not only to God perfectly but to all of God's children as well.

This is why Christianity is not just one creed among many. For love we have all been created. From where one comes, to what religion (if any) one currently adheres, the color of one's skin or gender or any of all the other myriad factors of being human are all desired in Christ (cf. Gal 3:28). This is why Christianity is the most "democratic" creed ever, excluding no one and desiring everyone.

This claim is neither naïve nor paternalistic but rather an argument that the essence of the human person is to love and to be loved. Everything else is "extra." As the Christian story goes, such

3 Maximus the Confessor, *On the Divine Names*, IV,4, in *Roots of Christian Mysticism*, trans. Olivier Clément (Hyde Park, NY: New City Press, 1995), 22.

intimacy was immediate in the Garden of Eden, but we lost it through sin. However, to quote the ancient Exultet you might hear at the Easter Vigil—*O Felix Culpa*—"O Happy Fault of Adam." Though at first Adam's rebellion cost all his progeny the divine life God intended, His Son's humanity has brought us something even better: divine union.

This call to union should also teach us that Christianity is not primarily an ethical code or a manual for a more virtuous life. Christianity is above all an encounter with a person who claims to be the consubstantial Son of God the Father, the one whose Body and Blood, now united with all human flesh, was crucified and rose again "on the third day" in order to sanctify—nay, to deify—our own flesh and blood.

With any act of union, we can ask: What brings Christ and Christian together? What is the glue between you and Jesus? The answer is the Holy Spirit, the one who effects any communion of true love. Eternally, the Holy Spirit is the Love between the Father and the Son, the Love between the eternal Lover and the eternally Beloved. Therefore, if the Holy Spirit's timeless role is to be the Love who glues together the Father and the Son from all time, would we not expect the first indication of the Spirit's role in our own lives to be that of "gluing" us to those whom we love? The conviction of sin is only a prelude, a preparation for the really important work to follow. We cannot enjoy the blossoming of a flower until we clear the soil of the weeds that will no doubt choke it. The Holy Spirit convicts of sin only to enable us to commune with persons human, angelic, and divine.

This week will be a very concrete look at the desires of our hearts and those whom we love. This is hopefully going to be a very incarnate time, in that those God has put into our lives as family and friends, neighbors and coworkers, are precisely the people through whom God has chosen to love us and exactly in whom He wants us to love Him. Do not over spiritualize your spiritual life: God is "happening" in every desire of your heart and revealing a bit more of

Himself in every act of charity you undertake, even for the "least" of your brothers and sisters.

Take some time to pray over photos from your phone or an old album of the people you love. These are the faces through whom the Father has loved you and to whom the Spirit has united you.

Where have you led another astray in the name of "love"? Is there anything you can still do to rectify that?

Christianity insists we love all people the way we love our own spouse and child(ren). Are you able to pray for that grace, including love for those you do not naturally like or might even consider an enemy?

The Church Fathers highlight the Holy Spirit's life as one of unity. For example, we can hear the martyred bishop of Antioch, Ignatius—as he is being dragged to Rome to be tortured to death in 107—encourage the Christians in Ephesus to see themselves as hewed stones that, although once dead, are being raised heavenward by the cable which is the Holy Spirit: "Deaf as stones you were: yes, stones for the Father's Temple, stones trimmed ready for God to build with, hoisted up by the derrick of Jesus Christ—the Cross—with the Holy Spirit for a cable; your faith being the winch which draws you up to God, up the ramp of love."[4] The Holy Spirit is Life-giving

4 Ignatius of Antioch, *Epistle to the Ephesians* §9, in *Early Christian*

union, the means by which we become one with another as well as become more and more integrated around the good ourselves.

Holiness thus stems from the word *wholeness*, as integrity comes from integer, a whole number. The Holy Spirit longs to dwell in and mend the divided heart. When we are divided against the Spirit of God and the spirit of the world, we shall never know who we are and we shall never be happy. The divided heart will never get what it wants because it wants two opposing things. Union is needed and a choice must be made. We all want to be happy, but then the pressing question arises: On whose terms can I be happy, through my own will or by following God's will for me? As a young man, Augustine struggled with his sexual urges and prayed to the Lord, "Grant me chastity and self-control, but please not yet!"[5] Did he really want to be chaste? How might God answer such a prayer? Do you ever pray like this—"Lord, your will be done . . . but here is what I need you to do for me"?

Since the Fall, only two humans have been wholly whole: the New Adam, by nature, and the New Eve, by grace. As perfect God and man, Jesus Christ not only reveals who God is but perfectly models who we too can be. Mary of course assimilated this perfection from the first moment of her existence. As the Spirit united these two at the Annunciation, Christ now wants to share that same spiritualization to us, enfleshed through His sacred flesh. As iron takes on the glow and heat of fire, those who draw near to Christ will begin to take on His properties and personality as well:

> How could humanity on earth, enslaved by death, recover its wholeness? It was necessary to give to dead flesh the ability to share in the life-giving power of God. Now the life-giving power of God is the Word, the only Son. He it was then whom God sent to us as Savior and Liberator. . . . He, though he is Life by nature, took a body subject to decay in order to destroy in it the power of death and transform it into life. As iron

Writings, trans. Maxwell Staniforth (New York: Penguin Books, 1987), 63.

5 Augustine, *Confessions* 8.7.17, trans. Maria Boulding (Hyde Park, NY: New City Press, 1997), 198.

> when it is brought in contact with fire immediately begins to share its color, so the flesh when it has received the life-giving Word into itself is set free from corruption. Thus he put on our flesh to set it free from death.[6]

As heat is what unites the flame with the iron, the Spirit is who unites Christ to Christian. Similarly, just as the iron does not lose its nature but now becomes something malleable, workable, and useful when placed in the fire, the human soul becomes what it can be united to Christ in the Spirit. In so doing, we regain our rightful place in creation: in the Spirit we are no longer led by our fallen biological instincts—given over into anger, lust, or gluttony—and instead live on the plane of those made in God's own image.

> Love, then, will see to it that we are conformed to God and, having been conformed and configured by him and cut off from this world, that we are not confused with the things that ought to be subject to us. But this is done by the Holy Spirit. For the apostle says, *Hope does not produce confusion, since the love of God has been poured into our hearts by the Holy Spirit who has been given to us* (Rom 5:5). In no way, however, could we be restored to wholeness by the Holy Spirit if he himself did not always remain whole and immutable. He could not do this, of course, unless he were the nature and substance of God. . . . The Holy Spirit does this for us. He is not a creature, therefore, because everything that exists is either God or a creature.[7]

> The One whom the Father has sent into our hearts, the Spirit of his Son, is truly God. Consubstantial with the Father and the Son, the Spirit is inseparable from them, in both the inner life of the Trinity and his gift of love for the world. In adoring the Holy Trinity, life-giving, consubstantial, and indivisible, the Church's faith also professes the distinction of persons. When the Father sends his Word, he always sends his Breath.

---

6 Cyril of Alexandria, Homily on Luke, V.19, in *Roots of Christian Mysticism*, 47.

7 Augustine, *The Catholic Way of Life* 1.23, in *The Manichean Debate*, trans. Roland Teske (Hyde Park, NY: New City Press, 2006), 42.

> In their joint mission, the Son and the Holy Spirit are distinct but inseparable. To be sure, it is Christ who is seen, the visible image of the invisible God, but it is the Spirit who reveals him. (CCC 689)

> When we begin to feel in its fullness the love of God, we begin also to love our neighbor in the experience of the Holy Spirit. That is the love of which the scriptures speak. For friendship according to the flesh breaks down too easily on the slightest pretext. The reason is that it lacks the bond of the Spirit. . . . But if a human friendship has been set ablaze again by the fire of divine love, it seeks with great joy to love its neighbor, even if in return it should have to undergo wrongs or insults. In fact, the bitterness of the quarrel can be wholly consumed in the sweetness of God.[8]

Since you started this retreat, has your understanding of the Holy Spirit changed at all? How so?

Are you better able to distinguish how Christ works in your life and where the Holy Spirit is found and what He is doing?

When you imagine yourself being drawn into the holy flame who is the Holy Spirit, what can you see being burned away, and what might be more mightily illumined in your life?

---

8 Diadochus of Photike, *Gnostic Chapters* §15, in *Roots of Christian Mysticism*, 279.

The Latin word *vulnera* means "wound." A paradoxical part of communion is vulnerability, the literal ability to be wounded. Communion demands that we, as the saying goes, "put ourselves out there." Communion is risky, but once again, the Trinity provides a pattern and a promise of what we too should be about.

To understand this rich piece of theology, let us return to the greatest and most influential Church Father, Saint Augustine of Hippo. Saint Augustine left the Church more writings than any other theologian of the first centuries, almost 5.5 million words in all. His treatises, biblical commentaries, and sermons are still subjects of lengthy studies, and his voice continues to teach the Church how to follow Christ more closely. Among all his contributions, his work on the Trinity is among his greatest achievements.

Begun around 400 and lasting for the next fifteen years or so, Augustine worked on a study simply entitled *On the Trinity*. Here he coins an image and a term, "substantial relationship," which is used to describe how close the unity is between the Father, Son, and Holy Spirit. Augustine borrows this language from the Greek philosopher Aristotle (d. 322 BC) who distinguished between what a thing essentially is—its "substance"—and the various properties that inhere in that thing, and which change and are altered over time and place—which Aristotle called "accidents." What Aristotle advances here is nothing more than common sense explained in philosophical language. You and I are substantially what we are our entire lives—human persons, men or women—and while we certainly do change, we do not change "substantially" but only "accidentally"; that is, we grow, we move locations, we age and get grey and gain weight, and all the other ways we are altered but stay essentially the same. It was common sense, but Aristotle helped us see that what a thing is (its substance) is separate from the various properties of that substance that can change without destroying what that thing essentially is (its accidents). For instance: we are all aging, perhaps graying, we can all stand and sit, and many other (accidental) changes that do not alter in any way the heart of who I am as a human person (my substance).

When you meet someone for the first time, you could ask them, "What are you?" That person would surely look at you with suspicion, thinking you might not be all there, but he would eventually answer, "I am a man, a human person." But if you wanted to take this encounter to the next level, you would ask this man, "But who are you?" Then the real conversation can begin. Now you can begin to get to know this man, know his history and hopes for his future, and so on, details of this person's life eventually unfolding. It is sort of like that with God. We can distinguish between "what" God is and "who" God is. As "God," we know He is the ultimate being above all and in all, and we can know a lot of things about God through what He has created (cf. Rom 1:18–20). But if we really want to enter into a deeper intimacy with God, we should really ask, "Who are you?" The answer the Christian hears is this: "I am the Father, I am the Son, and I am the Holy Spirit." "But since the Father is only called so because he has a Son, and the Son is only called so because he has a Father . . . but not said by way of a modification because what is signified by calling them Father and Son belongs to them eternally and unchangeably. Therefore, although being Father is different from being Son, there is no difference of substance, because they are not called these things substance-wise but relationship-wise; and yet this relationship is not a modification, because it is not changeable."[9]

For you who have been blessed with children: Did you change once your child was conceived? A bit, surely, but you remained substantially who you were before kids. As much as you love your children, the entirety of your personal identity does not depend on your sons and daughters. Your children have changed you accidentally. But it is not that way with God. In order for the Father to be who He is as Father, He must have a Son. The Father's entire distinctiveness requires another outside of Himself; it requires a relationship.

Augustine used this distinction between substance and accidents to explain how God is simply one and indivisible, immutable

[9] Augustine, *On the Trinity* 5.6, in *The Trinity*, 192.

and thus immune to partitioning or distinction or change. That is, there can be no accidents in the perfect Being. So, how can there be three divine Persons literally distinct from one another? Augustine answers:

> But now it is not one thing that makes him great and another that makes him God; what makes him great is what makes him God, because for him it is not one thing to be great and another to be God; so it will follow, presumably, that the Father is not God taken singly, but only with and taken together with the godhead he has begotten; and so the Son will be the godhead of the Father. . . . And furthermore, because it is not one thing for him to be and another for him to be God, it follows that the Son will also be the being of the Father, just as he is his Word and his image. This means that apart from being Father, the Father is nothing but what the Son is for him. It is clear, of course, that he is only called Father because he has a Son, since he is called Father not with reference to himself but with reference to the Son.[10]

The Father cannot be who He is without a Son. Therefore, the Son is how the Father is "Father," and the Father is how the Son is "Son," and the same goes for the Holy Spirit in between them.

Far from abstract dogma, this insight reveals an incredible paradox: The Persons of the Trinity are more dependent upon others than we are. The relationships in our lives change us, surely, but only a bit and surely not entirely. We remain human even though family members, friends, colleagues, and teachers have come in and out of our lives. Reliance upon others, these relationships and the vulnerability involved in allowing ourselves to depend on another, is not an imperfection but actually a divine perfection. The Persons of the Trinity thus model for us, made in the image and likeness of the Father, Son, and the Holy Spirit, that the fullness of life consists in self-gift and the joys of communion that follow the virtuous.

---

10 Augustine, *On the Trinity* 7.1, in *The Trinity*, 218.

Have you ever thought of the Persons of the Trinity depending on one another to be who They are? What images or fruits come to mind when you ponder this?

Have you experienced the relationship between love and vulnerability? How and with whom?

What scares you about becoming wholly open before another? Do you see this as something you are being called to and how you can imitate the Trinity?

What do you still "hide" from those with whom you feel the closest? What are you afraid of sharing?

Think again of the difference between a human parent and God the Father. A human mother or father had an identity well before they conceived a child—before that child ever came into the womb, his mother was already a daughter, a student, a friend, a community member, and so on. This woman's motherhood was a change "accidentally," in that it left her basic nature well intact. Yet it is not that way with God the Father, whose entire identity is contingent upon the fact that He begets a Son. Without a Son, why would we know the first Person of the Trinity as Father? Yet we do because the Son's begetting is eternal and connatural with what it means to be Father.

Imagine that! The Father is more dependent on another person than you and I are. If it were not for the Son, the Father could in no way be "Father." If it were not for the Father, the Son could not be "Son." Therefore, without that eternal bond between the Father and the Son, between the eternal Lover and Beloved, the Love who is the Holy Spirit would also be non-existent. This personal interdependence is who God is, an amazing insight into the power of personal relations. The only "difference" between the Father and the Son is the former Begets and the latter is Begotten. One is the One from whom all things come and the other is the One in whom that fullness is received; accordingly, that which is perfectly and timelessly shared is the Holy Spirit, that Gift binding the Giver and the Receiver.

Have you ever considered your dependence on your most beloved a perfection?

Is there anything that scares you about being so vulnerable? Do you allow yourself to be?

When we enter into communion with another, we inevitably change. This is why it is essential to pay attention to the company one keeps, for we become like those with whom we spend the most time. We humans soak up our surroundings, for better or for worse. We become friends with those we see, as the Ancients used to say, are our "other selves."

> What is the purpose of the Incarnation of the divine Logos which is proclaimed throughout the Scriptures, about which we read and which yet we do not recognize? Surely it is that he has shared in what is ours so as to make us participants of what is his. For the Son of God became the Son of Man in order to make us human beings sons and daughters of God, raising us up by grace to what he is by nature, giving us a new birth in the Holy Spirit and leading us directly into the kingdom of heaven. Or, rather, he gives us the grace to possess this kingdom of heaven within ourselves (cf. Lk 17:21), so that not merely do we hope to enter it but, being in full possession of it, we can affirm: "Our life is hid with Christ in God" (Col 3:3).[11]

The incarnate Son is never acquisitive or greedy about God's love but is born, lives, and lays His life down so others may know God as Father. Yet one Son was not enough for the Father; He yearns for countless sons and daughters, and so through Christ, Christians are able to be reborn in order to enjoy the divine life: "For this is to change what you had been, and to begin to be what you were not, that is, sons and daughters of God by grace, that the divine birth might shine forth in you, that the godly discipline might respond to God, the Father, that in the honor and praise of living, God may be glorified in man."[12] This divine adoption process is entirely Christ's doing. God can be glorified in men and women only because God's glory first became human. By taking on our sinful flesh, Jesus Christ not only redeems but renews.

---

11 Simeon the New Theologian, "Practical and Theological Preçepts," *The Philokalia* no. 108, in Nikodimos of the Holy Mountan and St. Makarios of Corinth, eds., *The Philokalia*, vol. IV, trans. G. E. H. Palmer, Philip Sherrard, and Kallistos Ware (London: Faber and Faber, 1998), 48. The *Philokalia*, literally "the love of the beautiful," is a collection of Greek theological texts and aphorisms, ranging from the fourth through the fifteenth century, started by Nikodimos (d. 1809) and Makarios (d. 1805) in the late 1700s.

12 Cyprian, *On Jealousy and Envy* §15, New Advent translation, https://www.newadvent.org/fathers/050710.htm.

The Spirit empowers Jesus to share His Father with us. He is never stingy or sparse in giving: in uniting the divine nature to our humanity, Jesus gives us His own Father, and from the cross, He gives us His own Mother as our own: "But when the fullness of time had come, God sent his Son, born of a woman, born under the law, to ransom those under the law, so that we might receive adoption. As proof that you are children, God sent the spirit of his Son into our hearts, crying out, 'Abba, Father!'" (Gal 4:4–6). "When Jesus saw his mother and the disciple there whom he loved, he said to his mother, 'Woman, behold, your son.' Then he said to the disciple, 'Behold, your mother.' And from that hour the disciple took her into his home" (Jn 19:26–27).

When we begin to think about Christianity as adoption into Jesus's own life and larger set of relationships, we can start to put the law in perspective and focus more on the unconditional love a perfect Father and Son and Spirit would have for an orphan they chose to adopt. Think of sin as a pitiful rebellion against your being adopted—it might be easier in the orphanage where no one asks where you have been or what you have been doing. There is an accountability in being adopted, and now there are a new set of eyes on you, a new set of expectations, a new identity for you to own. That is why our growth in holiness is more a matter of surrendering than achieving. The grace of God will make us godly, and we simply have to let that happen by trusting and conducting our lives as Christ's own:

> As now by participation in the Son of God one is adopted as a son or daughter, and by participating in that wisdom which is in God is rendered wise, so also by participation in the Holy Spirit is a man rendered holy and spiritual. For it is one and the same thing to have a share in the Holy Spirit, which is the Spirit of the Father and the Son, since the nature of the Trinity is one and incorporeal. And what we have said regarding the participation of the soul is to be understood of angels and heavenly powers in a similar way as of souls, because every rational creature needs a participation in the Trinity.[13]

---

[13] Origen, *On First Principles,* IV.32, New Advent translation, https://www.newadvent.org/fathers/04124.htm.

> He who justifies is the same who deifies because by justifying he made men into children of God: he gave them power to become children of God (Jn 1:12). If we are made God's children, we are made gods: but this is through the grace of the one who adopts and not through the nature of the one who begets. For there is only one Son of God: our Lord and Savior Jesus Christ. . . . The rest who have been made into gods are thus made by his grace and not born from his own substance, so as to be what he is, but they come to him through his generosity and are thus Christ's coheirs.[14]

Do you now see how we can be children of God and in truth call Him "Father," yet profess in the Creed that Jesus is "the only begotten Son of God"? Jesus is the "only" Son by nature, as eternal and as divine as the Father and the Holy Spirit. Yet in His generosity, He opens up these relationships to His Father and Spirit to us (and in time, His Mother—or as Vatican II put it, "our Mother in the order of grace"),[15] adopting us as new members of His heavenly household. This is never to denigrate our natural origins and our natural father and mother and family members, but it is to admit that our DNA does not save us. While some religions have one look back at family and land and heredity, Christianity has us look ahead at the promises of a new family, a new history, and a new life in Christ; in many important ways, the past is precisely that—the past. Whereas the Old Covenant was based on human blood, the

---

14 Augustine, *Expositions of the Psalms* 49.2, in *Expositions of the Psalms*, trans. Maria Boulding (Hyde Park, NY: New City Press, 2000), 381(emphasis in original).

15 Vatican Council II, Dogmatic Constitution *Lumen Gentium* (November 21, 1964), no. 61: "She conceived, brought forth and nourished Christ. She presented Him to the Father in the temple, and was united with Him by compassion as He died on the Cross. In this singular way she cooperated by her obedience, faith, hope and burning charity in the work of the Saviour in giving back supernatural life to souls. Wherefore she is our mother in the order of grace."

New Covenant is founded on the blood of God, the sacrifice of Jesus Christ that makes us members of His family.

Have you ever felt guilty for feeling closer to your faithful Christian friends than members of your own biological family? How do you pray about that?

Have you ever stopped and appreciated how generous and how patient Jesus and Mary are with you? How many times have you interrupted or even put off a prayer because of something else needing your attention? How many trivial things do we make more time for than we do for these two?

How would any other relationship go if we treated somebody else the way we do Jesus and Mary?

Are you ever tempted into thinking that being a son or daughter will mean an easy life? It means eternal joy, for sure, but how do you reconcile belonging to God and still being asked to suffer and carry your cross? Does it help that even Jesus had to learn in this manner: "Son though he was, he learned obedience from what he suffered" (Heb 5:8)? What might this mean for you and your life circumstances?

At the section of the *Catechism* explaining the line in the Creed, "He was conceived by the power of the Holy Spirit, and born of the Virgin," the Church enlists some of her greatest theologians to explain how:

> The Word became flesh to make us "partakers of the divine nature" (2 Pet 1:4): "For this is why the Word became man, and the Son of God became the Son of man: so that man, by entering into communion with the Word and thus receiving divine sonship, might become a son of God" (St. Irenaeus)" "For the Son of God became man so that we might become God" (St. Athanasius). "The only-begotten Son of God, wanting to make us sharers in his divinity, assumed our nature, so that he, made man, might make men gods" (St. Thomas Aquinas). (CCC 460)

It is hard for us moderns to appreciate the depth of this teaching, thinking it sounds rather heretical at first. The key word in understanding is scriptural. In the Spirit and as other sons and daughters of the Father, we "participate" in the divine nature. This means that the divinity that perfects our humanity is never ours. We partake of God the way iron partakes of fire, or how someone can partake of a conversation, show, or some other event which changes them but which they can never call their own. That is humanity's primal temptation, to "possess" the divine nature and think that we are godly on our own, apart from God. In their pride, Adam and Eve sought to steal divinity on their own terms: "You will be like Gods" (Gn 3:5).

In the "kenotic hymn" of Philippians 2 (*kenotic* from the Greek word *kenosis*, meaning "empty," "like a cenotaph," "an empty tomb") Jesus shows us how not to grasp at divinity on our terms but to receive it from the Father. This is the heart of Saint Paul's theology, proclaiming a God who although infinitely rich, "yet for your sake he became poor, so that by his poverty you might become rich" (2 Cor 8:9). This is the great exchange of God's humanity for our divinity, His emptying of Himself so we might be able to be filled with the Son:

> Who, though he was in the form of God, did not count equality with God a thing to be grasped, but emptied himself, taking the form of a servant, being born in the likeness of men. And being found in human form he humbled himself and became obedient unto death, even death on a cross. Therefore God has highly exalted him and bestowed on him the name which is above every name, that at the name of Jesus every knee should bow, in heaven and on earth and under the earth, and every tongue confess that Jesus Christ is Lord, to the glory of God the Father. (Phil 2:5–11)

Using the image of Isaiah's imperfections being purged and his godliness being strengthened by the angel's touching of a heated coal to his lips (cf. Is 6:6), John of Damascus wants us to pray for that same grace which rebirths the divine image in us, renewing in us the grace that makes us like God: "Let us receive the divine burning coal, so that the fire of the coal may be added to the desire within us to consume our sins and enlighten our hearts, and so that by this communion of the divine fire we may be set afire and deified."[16]

What mortal would not want this promise? Do we all not desire perfection, eternal joy, and intimate communion with our loved ones that will never end? Do we not long for all the best experiences we can only now imagine to last forever? Who would not want to be "pure and incorrupt" as John maintains? This is what is promised in Christ, but it is a promise from Him and cannot be had without Him. This is why the Church Fathers never tire of teaching us that we remain aloof from any real happiness and integrity until we allow ourselves to be drawn into the fire of the Spirit and the Body of the Son.

This is a promise we need not wait until heaven to know. We are not only able to live as God's children, as citizens of heaven here on earth, but we have the baptismal vocation to do so. A Christian is not mere terrestrial, no mere American or Republican or Democrat.

---

16 John of Damascus, *On the Orthodox Faith* 4.13, in *St. John of Damascus: Writings*, trans. Frederic Chase (Washington, DC: Catholic University of America Press, 1958), 359.

We are children of the Father, and we must resist the temptation to be enticed and enchanted into thinking this life is for power and success, while only in heaven do we need to worry about things like mercy and love of enemy. We can make this mistake in the big picture (earth now, heaven later), or we are probably more tempted to do it on a more micro level: "God stuff" on Sunday, "world stuff" throughout the work week.

The Eucharist must be the antidote against such a spiritual division. Jesus Christ is still here, His Apostles still teach, His priests still offer sacrifice, His saints still heal and speak in tongues and challenge Caesar's authority in the world. For whenever we avail ourselves of the Blessed Sacrament—whether at Holy Communion or during Eucharistic Adoration—we are being deified and invited into a living incorruptibility, even while in this ephemeral world.

> The Eucharist unites the body, as Baptism the soul, to God. Our bodies, having received poison, need an Antidote; and only by eating and drinking can it enter. One Body, the receptacle of Deity, is this Antidote, thus received. But how can it enter whole into each one of the Faithful? This needs an illustration. Water gives its own body to a skin-bottle. So nourishment (bread and wine) by becoming flesh and blood gives bulk to the human frame: the nourishment is the body. Just as in the case of other men, our Saviour's nourishment (bread and wine) was his Body; but these, nourishment and Body, were in him changed into the Body of God by the Word indwelling. So now repeatedly the bread and wine, sanctified by the Word (the sacred Benediction), is at the same time changed into the Body of that Word; and this Flesh is disseminated among all the Faithful.[17]

> To what hope the Lord has called us, what we now carry about with us, what we endure, what we look forward to, is well known. . . . We carry mortality about with us, we endure infirmity, we look forward to divinity. For God wishes not only to

---

[17] Gregory of Nyssa, *Catechetical Oration* 37, New Advent translation, https://www.newadvent.org/fathers/2908.htm.

> vivify, but also to deify us. When would human infirmity ever have dared to hope for this, unless divine truth had promised it? Still, it was not enough for our God to promise us divinity in himself, unless he also took on our infirmity, as though to say, "Do you want to know how much I love you, how certain you ought to be that I am going to give you my divine reality? I took to myself your mortal reality." We mustn't find it incredible, brothers and sisters, that human beings become gods, that is, that those who were human beings become gods.[18]

The promise of our glory is paradoxically found in Christ's ingloriousness. His humility, rejection, and consequent death are all ways of showing us that we "are not far from the kingdom of God" (Mk 12:34). For we might not yet know resurrection and beatitude, we do know what it means to be a stumbling human trying to make sense of it all. This is why Christ shows His wounds, this is why He comes to us gently and humbly, quietly and without pyrotechnics and thunder, so we who are mortal and limited can finally rest assured that God is near.

Yet He ever remains God. Even though the heresy of Arianism, which subordinated the Son to the Father, was condemned by Saint Athanasius and other orthodox bishops at the Council of Nicaea, the work of insisting on Christ's divinity was not over. Athanasius used Jesus's consubstantiality with the Father to show how the One who deifies is not in need of deification but promises that to us instead. Furthermore, just as the Holy Spirit unites Christ's divine and human nature perfectly, He also unifies the Christian with the Church, manifesting His consubstantiality as well:

> So, then, in the Spirit the Word glorifies creatures and after he has divinized them and made them sons and daughters of God, he leads them to the Father. But that which joins creatures to the Word cannot be a creature. And that which makes creatures sons and daughters cannot be foreign to the Son. Otherwise another spirit would be needed by which this

[18] Augustine, *Sermon* 23B.1, in Edmund Hill, *Sermons: Newly Discovered Sermons* (Hyde Park, NY: New City Press, 1997), 37.

> Spirit could be joined to the Word. But this is absurd. And so, the Spirit is not one of the things that has come into existence, but is proper to the divinity of the Father. In him the Word divinizes all that has come into existence. And the one in whom creatures are divinized cannot himself be external to the divinity of the Father.[19]

Empowered with the eternal insight of who this Spirit is, then, Jesus in the New Testament reveals the Spirit with some slightly different imagery. We were already with the Holy Spirit as fire, but we first meet Him in the New Covenant as the One who quietly "overshadows" Mary at the Annunciation:

> Then the angel said to her, "Do not be afraid, Mary, for you have found favor with God. Behold, you will conceive in your womb and bear a son, and you shall name him Jesus. He will be great and will be called Son of the Most High, and the Lord God will give him the throne of David his father, and he will rule over the house of Jacob forever, and of his kingdom there will be no end." But Mary said to the angel, "How can this be, since I have no relations with a man?" And the angel said to her in reply, "The Holy Spirit will come upon you, and the power of the Most High will overshadow you. Therefore the child to be born will be called holy, the Son of God." (Lk 1:30–35)

The Holy Spirit's overshadowing of Mary is continued in what is called the "epiclesis" of the Catholic Mass. This occurs when the priest extends his hands over the bread and wine and calls (*klesis*) the Holy Spirit down (*epi*) upon these gifts now offered on the altar. This invocation, or "coming down," is how we met the Holy Spirit at Pentecost, a feast which is extended through every Mass.

Pray over this passage of Luke 1:30–35. Slowly read the passage again and ask yourself these questions: (1) What was Mary

[19] Athanasius, *Letter to Serapion* 1.25.5, in *Works on the Spirit: Athanasius and Didymus,* trans. Mark DelCogliano et al (Yonkers, NY: St. Vladimir's Seminary Press, 2011), 90–91.

afraid of, and what most scares me? (2) Do I ever look at God and ask that same question of Mary, "How can this be?"

Do I trust the Lord loves me and is providentially inviting me each day into greater union, into greater love?

Do I ever imagine Jesus in me at the time of Holy Communion continuing Mary's call to carry Jesus in her very self as well?

Did you pick up on this? If you are Catholic, this is an amazing insight (and if you're not, bear with us). Jesus Christ is God-made-flesh; every Christian knows that. This same Jesus Christ also promised never to leave us orphans (see Jn 14:18) and that He would be with us always, even to the end of time (see Mt 28:20). If that is true, and Christ cannot lie, where is this incarnate Messiah, where is this enfleshed God? The ancient Christian answer is: in the Holy Eucharist, of course. That same incarnation which occurred two thousand years ago—changing all of history and humankind forever—continues today just down the street from you.

That is, the same Holy Spirit who descended upon Mary's womb continues to "overshadow" that which is natural and impersonal (bread and wine) in order to transform it into a supernatural person. In this encounter, through the "binding" power of the Spirit's overshadowing, humanity and divinity become one. The flesh of Mary is converted—transubstantiated—into the flesh of the living God. In the celebration of the Mass, Jesus's promise to be with us always is thus continued: at the epiclesis, the Holy Spirit descends upon the natural elements of bread and wine and as the Church will hear shortly thereafter in Jesus's own words, "This is my Body," "This is my Blood." Just like at the Annunciation itself, there is no fanfare, no trumpet blast, just a receptive Bride (Mary, the Church, you) saying "yes," praying "amen," allowing the Lord to yet again enter into His creation, into the life of a disciple, a friend, a lover.

The Eucharist created the Church; the Bride came forth from the Groom pierced on the cross. The Body of Christ is now found in the Body of Christ, the Savior in the Sacrament, and that is the mainstay of any truly Catholic theology. As early as 107, there were already bishops pleading with their flock to keep themselves in a state of grace so they can celebrate the Real Presence with clear consciences and thus receive the "medicine of immortality" which is the Body and Blood of Jesus in the worship of His one, holy, catholic, and apostolic Church: "They even absent themselves from the Eucharist and the public prayers, because they will not admit that the Eucharist is the self-same body of our Savior Jesus Christ which suffered for our sins, and which the Father in his goodness raised up again."[20] "I hope to write you a further letter . . . man by man and name by name, attending your meetings in a state of grace, united in faith and in Jesus Christ (who is the seed of David according to the flesh, and is the Son of Man and Son of God), and are ready now to obey your bishop and clergy with undivided minds and to share in the one common breaking of Bread, the medicine of immortality, and the sovereign remedy by which we escape death and live in Jesus Christ for evermore."[21]

The first apologist, Justin Martyr, so called for his writings to the Roman government defending the intelligence and civic loyalty of Christians, held very early on that the Eucharist is not only the Body and Blood of Jesus Christ—which no ancient Christian disputed—but that we are to assimilate and so become that divine presence as well:

---

20 Ignatius of Antioch, *Letter to the Smyrnaeans* §7, in *Early Christian Writings*, 102.

21 Ignatius of Antioch, *Letter to the Ephesians* §20, in *Early Christian Writings*, 66.

> We call this food the Eucharist, of which only he can partake who has acknowledged the truth of our teachings, who has been cleansed by baptism for the remission of his sins and for his regeneration, and who regulates his life upon the principles laid down by Christ. Not as ordinary bread or as ordinary drink do we partake of them, but just as, through the word of God, our Savior Jesus Christ became Incarnate and took upon himself flesh and blood for our salvation, so, we have been taught, the food which has been made the Eucharist by the prayer of his word, and which nourishes our flesh and blood by assimilation, is both the flesh and blood of that Jesus who was made flesh.[22]

As the Church entered further and further into the Greco-Roman world, a heftier defense had to be made for the human person as both body and soul. The prevailing philosophy of the time was much like the scene today: to be human meant you were just a soul whose body was incidental and thus manipulable, if not disposable.

> Now, the blood of the Lord is twofold: one is corporeal, redeeming us from corruption; the other is spiritual, and it is with that we are anointed. To drink the blood of Jesus is to participate in his incorruption. . . . Similarly, wine is mixed with water and the Spirit is joined to man: the first, the mixture, provides feasting that faith may be increased; the other, the Spirit, leads us on to incorruption. The union of both, that is, of the portion and the Word, is called the Eucharist, a gift worthy of praise and surpassingly fair; those who partake of it are sanctified in body and soul, for it is the will of the Father that man, a composite made by God, be united to the Spirit and to the Word.[23]

---

22 Justin Martyr, *First Apology* 66, *Saint Justin Martyr: The Writings*, trans., Thomas Falls (Washington, DC: Catholic University of America Press, 2008), 105–6.

23 Clement of Alexandria, *Christ the Educator* II.2.19, in *Christ the Educator*, trans. Simon Wood (Washington, DC: Catholic University of America

> Therefore with fullest assurance let us partake as of the Body and Blood of Christ: for in the figure of the bread is given to you his Body, and in the figure of wine his Blood; that you by partaking of Christ's Body and Blood, too might be made of the same body and blood with him. For thus we come to bear Christ in us, because his Body and Blood are diffused through our members; thus it is that, according to the blessed Peter that we have become "partakers of the divine nature."[24]

There are two lines of theological insight running through most of the Church Fathers' writings on the Eucharist: first, that what may appear to be just bread and wine (the "figure," as Cyril put it) are transformed into the living Body and Blood of Jesus Christ; and second, that this transformation is effected in order that we too become that same body and blood.

So, when you attend the sacred liturgy, come to Mass not as a spectator but as an offering. You and your life are to be placed on the paten along with the bread, in the chalice along with the wine. Even though the priest is instructed to pray this *sotto voce*, in a subdued voice, he prays this for you at every single Mass as you see him dribble just a drop of water into the wine-filled chalice: "By the mystery of this water and wine may we come to share in the divinity of Christ who humbled himself to share in our humanity." That is the prayer of the Mass, that as Christ became like us, we become like Him through the holy sacrifice re-presented directly in front of us, for us.

Prepare your hearts by studying the readings for that Mass, by reflecting on the prayers and possible prefaces for that Mass (all available online). For example, notice one of the Eucharistic Prayers where the priest prays: "Look, we pray, upon the oblation of your Church and, recognizing the sacrificial Victim by whose death you willed to reconcile us to yourself, grant that we, who are nourished

---

Press, 2008), 111.

[24] Cyril of Jerusalem, *Lectures on the Christian Sacraments* IV.3, in *St. Cyril of Jerusalem: Lectures on the Christian Sacraments*, trans. F. L. Cross (Crestwood, NY: St. Vladimir Seminary Press, 1995), 68, slightly adjusted.

by the Body and Blood of your Son and filled with his Holy Spirit, may become one body, one spirit in Christ. May he make of us an eternal offering to you, so that we may obtain an inheritance with your elect, especially with the most Blessed Virgin Mary, Mother of God, with your blessed Apostles and glorious Martyrs."

Heaven will not be filled with the celebration of Masses but with the celebrated masses of the saints! It is we who become that "eternal offering," and at the epiclesis of every Mass, we should pray that the Holy Spirit consecrates us as much as He does the bread and wine on the altar. Now one with Christ through Baptism, we too are offered to the Father in each sacrifice of the Mass, and so we pray that Christ may "make of us an eternal offering to" the Father. In so doing, we have been invited to become one with Christ, "one body, one spirit," as well as with "Mary, the Mother of God, with the blessed Apostles and glorious Martyrs," and all the saints. Could you imagine a greater invitation and way to spend your life?

Have you ever noticed the "epiclesis" at Mass? Do you truly believe that the incarnation of Christ continues, is in no way lessened, and is present for you in every Holy Communion? Do you make time to pray before the Blessed Sacrament? Could you find where the closest adoration times are near you?

Week 7

The Holy Spirit and Jesus's Church

We have just spent some time reflecting on the essence of Christianity as a love affair, a matter of intimate communion ultimately brought about by the Holy Spirit's uniting us to those we love and those who first loved us. In this communion, we cannot stay as we were; love naturally transforms, and love of God supernaturally deifies. That is, deification is not against our nature but above it; sin is unnatural, but love supernatural.

Where does this transformation take place? In the Church, which is the Body of Jesus Christ on earth. During this seventh week of Easter, we will focus in on our vocation as members of the Body of Christ. His Church, He promises, will forever be one, holy, catholic, and apostolic. This means that like His own incarnation, the Church will be both human and divine: divine in its stability and safeguard in proclaiming what is infallibly true, yet human in its reliance on sinful men and women to speak and act Christlike. Saint Cyprian saw this union symbolized at every Mass as the priest pours a drop of water into the wine: the water represents the weakness of human nature while the wine symbolizes the intoxicating power of God, and together these two form the Church: "And this bonding and union between water and wine in the Lord's cup is achieved in such a way that nothing can thereafter separate their intermingling. Thus there is nothing that can separate the union between Christ and the Church, that is, the people who are established within the Church and who steadfastly and faithfully persevere in their beliefs: Christ and his Church must remain ever attached and joined to each other by indissoluble love."[1]

This final week before the celebration of Pentecost Sunday, let us focus our prayers and thoughts on the nature and mission of the Church Jesus Christ founded and where the fullness of His presence can be found on earth. The readings this week are:

> John 17:1–11,
> John 17:11–19, or
> John 17:20–26.

These bring us into what is traditionally considered "the high priestly prayer" of Jesus. This week, it is as if we are blessed enough to eavesdrop on His dialogue with the Father. And as He knowingly and willingly goes to His death, what is on His mind? We are! We are His only concern, praying in order to prepare us for the battle in and against "the world." "And now I will no longer be in the world, and these are in the world, and I come to you. . . . I do not ask that you take them out of the world but that you keep them from the evil one. They do not belong to the world any more than I belong to the world. Consecrate them in the truth. Your word is truth. As you sent me into the world, so I sent them into the world. And I consecrate myself for them, so that they also may be consecrated in truth" (Jn 17:11, 15–19). Christ consecrates Himself for our communion as well as for our combat.

Before we can evangelize others, however, we must first let the love of Christ marinate our hearts in silent prayer and still contemplation, as "useless" or "unproductive" as the world might judge these to be. The Church is not a social work agency, as noble as that work

---

1 Cyprian, *Letter* 63.13.1, in *The Letters of St. Cyprian of Carthage*, trans. G. W. Clarke (Mahwah, NJ: The Newman Press, 1986), 105.

can be. The Church is first and foremost a school of love, and as we have seen, love unites and transforms.

In fact, we are taught this lesson at the first encounter on the first Easter morning. Before Mary Magdalene sets out, she first allows the Lord to orient her to their Father. Here we see adoption and deification at play: Mary is told that she and Jesus have the same Father but they are His child in two different ways. Jesus is Son by nature, she a daughter by grace: "My Father and your Father, to my God and your God"—same Father, same God, simply two different means of belonging and thus being "god." "Jesus said to her, 'Mary!' She turned and said to him in Hebrew, 'Rabbouni,' which means Teacher. Jesus said to her, 'Stop holding on to me, for I have not yet ascended to the Father. But go to my brothers and tell them, "I am going to my Father and your Father, to my God and your God."' Mary of Magdala went and announced to the disciples, 'I have seen the Lord,' and what he told her" (Jn 20:16–18).

Eternally, the Son is begotten of the Father without a mother; in time, however, the Son is begotten of Mary without a (human) father. Here the risen Christ insists that His disciples know that His God, His Father, is also their God and Father. Only three days earlier He had given us His mother from the cross: "When Jesus saw his mother and the disciple there whom he loved, he said to his mother, 'Woman, behold, your son.' Then he said to the disciple, 'Behold, your mother.' And from that hour the disciple took her into his home" (Jn 19:26–27).

You may have noticed that more traditional Catholics never refer to the Church as an "it" but refer to her as a "she." Like Mary, it is proper to refer to the Church as "mother," as "teacher." The Church is the living Bride of Christ, the one who washes us in the waters of Baptism, who welcomes us back through the gift of absolution, who like any loving mother feeds us and who is there when the time comes for us to leave this world.

This Bride is no mere building, not a cold code of ethics; it is neither clerical power nor magisterial teaching. The Church is Christ alive in you. This does not do away with the divinely-instituted sacraments and papacy and Sacred Tradition, but it is to say that all of those are means to one thing: your holiness!

The Church Fathers knew that this gathering of the saints was the sole and entire purpose of God's creating the universe. This is why God did anything outside of Himself, to create and gather a people who could enjoy life and enjoy it to the full (cf. Jn 10:10). That is why, quoting a third century work from Rome which is full of visions and ecstasies, the *Catholic Catechism* teaches:

> Christians of the first centuries said, "The world was created for the sake of the Church" (*Shepherd of Hermas*, Vision 2.4.1). God created the world for the sake of communion with his divine life, a communion brought about by the "convocation" of men in Christ, and this "convocation" is the Church. The Church is the goal of all things, and God permitted such painful upheavals as the angels' fall and man's sin only as occasions and means for displaying all the power of his arm and the whole measure of the love he wanted to give the world:
>
> Just as God's will is creation and is called "the world," so his intention is the salvation of men, and it is called "the Church." (CCC 760)

Again, why did God create? Why is there something rather than nothing? The Church, the Body of Christ, the gathering of those rejoicing and grateful for all God has brought into being. For when our joy is full, we realize that we have been created to be God's glory and that the fullness of life is being with Him forever. Or, in the beautiful words of Saint Irenaeus, "The glory of God is the human person fully alive, the life of man is to behold God."[2] Or as Saint John had written, our life will be one of eternal assimilation into God's own life: "We shall be like him, for we shall see him as he is" (1 Jn 3:2). This is the Church, this is the sole reason the Trinity decided to act outside of himself, the very purpose of God's creating.

---

2 Irenaeus, *Against the Heresies* IV.20.7, our translation; the Latin is most beautiful: "Gloria enim Dei vivens homo, vita autem hominis visio Dei."

Do you enjoy philosophical questions and discussions? Why or why not?

Have you ever thought about the ultimate purpose of this world?

Do you order your life toward one ultimate end or toward many intermediate ends only?

How do you understand "the Church"? How do you understand the connection between your obedience to Jesus and to His Church? What about your affection?

We live in a time of disconnect. As quickly as we can be in touch through electronic media, we are the first generation to establish an industry that thrives on autonomy and isolation. We now have the ability to watch a movie alone, never needing to leave home; we can eat dinner from our local restaurant alone, never needing to leave home; we can even "see" the doctor or therapist alone, never needing to leave home. This is not the way the human person can thrive. We were not made for isolation, yet everywhere we look, there are strong separations—politically, sexually, spiritually, economically.

But Jesus wants something more for us than this; He desires to bring what He has enjoyed eternally in the Trinity to each of us: interpersonal unity. This does not mean He is going to place us all in a convent or seminary. He needs us in the world, the world He loved so much that He came to die for it (see Jn 3:16). So, as we go about our daily, oftentimes uneventful lives, let us always remember Jesus's prayer to the Father with each of us in mind: "I pray for them. I do not pray for the world but for the ones you have given me, because they are yours, and everything of mine is yours and everything of yours is mine, and I have been glorified in them. And now I will no longer be in the world, but they are in the world, while I am coming to you. Holy Father, keep them in your name that you have given me, so that they may be one just as we are" (Jn 17:9–11).

This call for unity is a theme running throughout the Gospels, all of Saint Paul's letters, and certainly the earliest of the Christian apologists and Church Fathers. A bishop soon to be martyr, Ignatius of Antioch, stresses the visible unity effected by gathering around the one true Eucharist under the episcopal gaze of the bishop Christ has placed over his local flock:

> Every man who belongs to God and Jesus Christ stands by his bishop. As for the rest, if they repent and come back into the unity of the Church, they too shall belong to God, and so bring their lives into conformity with Jesus Christ. But make no mistake, my brothers, the adherents of a schismatic can never inherit the Kingdom of God. Those who wander in outlandish by-ways of doctrine must forfeit all part in the Lord's Passion. Make certain, therefore, that you all observe one common Eucharist, for there is but one Body of our Lord Jesus Christ, and but one cup of union with his Blood; and one altar of sacrifice—even also as there is but one bishop, with his clergy and my own fellow servitors the deacons. This will ensure that all your doings are in full accord with the will of God.[3]

---

3 Ignatius of Antioch, *Letter to the Philadelphians*, 3-4, in *Early Christian Writings*, trans. Maxwell Staniforth (New York: Penguin Books, 1987), 93–94.

In the next century, Origen will highlight how the unity Christ desires for His people is His way of helping us identify more and more with Him. It is impossible to unite with that which is still becoming or is, worse, fragmented. Union demands stability, and in Christ we come to a unity which does not destroy but in fact perfects our individuality:

> "One" has many meanings, including that of likeness. It is used both of harmony and likeness. "All the believers were of one mind" (Acts 4:32), and in the same way, "by one Spirit we were all baptized into one body" (1 Cor 12:13). According to likeness of nature and having Adam as the natural origin and head of our birth, we are all said to have one body. So also we are inscribed as having Christ as head through our new birth, which has become to us a figure of the death and resurrection of him who rose as the firstborn of the dead. We inscribe him as head according to the prefiguring of his resurrection, of whom we are individually members and a body through the Spirit, begotten unto incorruption.[4]

For the Christian, charity, unity, and likeness really are synonymous. Love without union is only fanciful infatuation; any attempt at union without love is only a relationship of utility or pleasure; and, finally, wherever there is love and unity, there will be a likeness of mind and heart. What was undone at the Tower of Babel is reunified at Pentecost. This is the restoration for which our isolation cries. In the biblical story of creation, humanity enjoys the strongest natural bond—for unlike all the other creatures, we are the only ones who originate not from a pair but from one, Adam. From him comes Eve, and from those two, the entire human race springs forth.

> When perfect love has driven out fear, or fear has been transformed into love, then everything that has been saved will be a unity growing together through the one and only Fullness,

---

[4] Origen, *Fragment 140 on the Gospel of John*, in *Ancient Christian Commentary on Scripture*, trans. Thomas Oden (Downers Grove, IL: InterVarsity Press, 2007), 245.

> and everyone will be, in one another, a unity in the perfect Dove, the Holy Spirit. . . . In this way, encircled by the unity of the Holy Spirit as the bond of peace, all will be one body and one spirit. . . . But it would be better to quote the very words of the Gospel literally: "That they may all be one; even as thou, Father, art in me and I in thee, that they also may be in us" (Jn 17:21). Now the bond of this unity is glory. And that this glory is the Holy Spirit, anyone familiar with Scripture will agree if he is attentive to the word of the Lord: "The glory which thou hast given me, I have given to them" (Jn 17:22). He has indeed really given them such glory when he said: "Receive the Holy Spirit" (Jn 20:22).[5]

The fragmentation our society is experiencing today was first experienced by the Tower of Babel in Genesis 11:1–9. This story was just one way the Jewish people captured the effects of sin in their time: disunity, chaos, a hubris that challenged God and made man think he could do whatever he wanted with no accountability. They would go on to experience the inevitable divisions such pride brings. But God is patient, God is merciful, and He did not want such pandemonium to be the last word. Once again, He slowly goes to work. Pentecost is the undoing of Babel, whose infamous tower has been refashioned into the Church. "And so, as they were staying in the city, on the day of Pentecost there came the Holy Spirit, filling the disciples; they spoke with the tongues of all nations. One person was speaking with the tongues of all nations, because the unity of the Church was going to come about in all nations."[6]

Out of many languages, there is a new kind of unforeseen unity. The Spirit binds and seeks to achieve a communion that tears down divisions and restores peace, peace between God and you, between

---

5 Gregory of Nyssa, *Homilies on the Song of Songs*, 15, in *Roots of Christian Mysticism*, trans. Olivier Clément (Hyde Park, NY: New City Press, 1995), 273.

6 Augustine, *Sermon* 229I.3, in *Sermons 184-229Z*, trans. Edmund Hill (New Rochelle, NY: New City Press, 1993), 301.

you and your neighbor, and even within your own psychic need for inner-harmony.

> But as the old confusion of tongues was laudable, when men who were of one language in wickedness and impiety, even as some now venture to be, were building the Tower; for by the confusion of their language the unity of their intention was broken up, and their undertaking destroyed; so much more worthy of praise is the present miraculous one. For being poured from One Spirit upon many men, it brings them again into harmony. And there is a diversity of Gifts, which stands in need of yet another Gift to discern which is the best, where all are praiseworthy.[7]

But what happens if we are asked why we personally do not speak in this way, in many languages or in the Spirit's gift of tongues?

> We must realize, brothers and sisters, that this Holy Spirit is who pours forth charity into our hearts. By this charity the Church of God was to be assembled from every corner of the globe. Now united by the Holy Spirt, the Church by her very unity speaks in every tongue, as then each recipient of the Holy Spirit spoke. If then anyone were to say to one of us, "You have received the Holy Spirit, why do you not speak in every tongue?," he ought to answer, "I do! For I am part of the Body of Christ, the Church, I mean, and she speaks in every tongue. . . ."
>
> Celebrate, then, this day as members of the Body of Christ. For you will not celebrate in vain, if you are what you celebrate by adhering together to that Church which God fills with the Holy Spirit; that Church which by her growth throughout the world he recognizes as his own and by which he in turn is recognized. . . . To you of every nation who constitute the Church of Christ, the members of Christ, the Body of Christ, the Spouse of Christ, to you it is that the Apostle says,

---

7 Gregory Nazianzen, *Oration* 41.16 ("On Pentecost"), New Advent translation, https://www.newadvent.org/fathers/310241.htm.

"Supporting one another in charity, careful to keep the unity of the Spirit in the bond of Peace" (Eph 4:2–3).[8]

Does your speech reflect your love of Jesus? Where could you purify your choice of words?

Where do you sense the most obvious unity in your life? With whom and why? Would you be able to be more conscious and intentional with this person or these people?

Do you see the absence of God in the world as the cause of disunity and fragmentation and chaos? Are you able to pray charitably here?

For the past two thousand years, Christ's Church has proven to be the most constant and consistent gathering of men and women ever—surviving persecutions, scandals, infidelities, and attacks of all sorts. The motto of the Carthusian Order of monks will always ring true: *Stat crux dum volvitur orbis,* "The Cross is steady while the world turns." The time of the late 1600s until around the early nineteenth century (symbolically dated at 1804 with the death of the philosopher Immanuel Kant) is now known as the Enlightenment, an era of great scientific advancements and globalization.

8 Fulgentius of Ruspe, *Sermon 8.2-3 on Pentecost,* in *Catholicism: Christ and the Common Destiny of Man,* trans. Henri DeLubac (San Francisco: Ignatius Press, [1947] 1988), 378–79.

During this time of supposed "sophistication," organized religion was downgraded into a personal and highly emotional affair. Despite the work of some wonderful theologians of this time, most of the intelligentsia in Europe and America began to view religion as a crutch for the weak, something devoid of intellectual rigor and importance for the wider public. Religious affairs therefore became a matter of personal opinion, of subjective doctrine open to myriads of interpretations all on par with each other. As Immanuel Kant famously remarked, "Whether we are to worship three or ten persons in the Deity makes no difference."

Sound familiar? This was the seedbed from where we find ourselves today—in a world where religious opinion is allowed as long as, first, you do not take it too seriously and, second, refuse to share what you believe with others, and certainly do not use it to influence public policy. Now, things as serious as the life of the unborn are degenerated into mere "opinion," and anyone who stands up for the most vulnerable is labeled a fanatic or an "extremist."

That is why we cannot fall into the trap of separating spirituality from doctrine as so many do today (especially professional "theologians"). Our growing devotion to the Holy Spirit is in proportion to our intelligent study and theological sophistication. This does not mean that you need to get to graduate school or begin to learn all the ancient languages. What it does mean is that you begin to trust that the Lord cannot only use but actually needs your surrender and subsequent availability.

First, we trust that the Holy Spirit is at work as we go throughout our day. We trust that His silence is even more eloquent than our words. We trust that simply by being available to do His will is the beginning of God's ability to rely on anything we might give Him. "For the holy Spirit will teach you at that moment what you should say" (Lk 12:12). This is to own the Christian reality that by the grace of Baptism, you have always lived in the Spirit and can begin to do so now more intentionally that He dwells in you. "Through the power of the Holy Spirit we take part in Christ's Passion by dying to sin, and in his Resurrection by being born to a new life; we are members of his Body which is the Church, branches grafted onto the vine which is himself: "[God] gave himself to us through his Spirit. By the participation of the Spirit, we become communicants in the divine nature. . . . For this reason, those in whom the Spirit dwells are divinized" (CCC 1988).[9]

It is to realize that you have a responsibility not only to live your life in accord with the Spirit but also to bring Him to others. This requires prayer, study, and a willingness to evangelize in ways proper to your life and state. One obvious way we show "the call we have received" is by how we treat one another. Christian action is very palpable and easy to "measure." Prayer and action are two indispensable modes of being Christian, but because the latter is easy to gauge, easier to see results, and so more tempting to feel good about, we must always search for a fruitful balance between the two. Activism cannot be the goal of Christianity, in that it is just as much about being a new creature as it is doing good toward others. Even someone as generous as Saint Augustine realized it was not his vocation to alleviate the perennial problem of poverty: "It's not the bishop's business to save up gold, and repulse the beggar's outstretched hand. There are so many asking every day, so many groaning, so many needy people pleading, that we have to leave several of them unhappy, because we haven't got enough to give all of them something."[10]

> Do you see yourself as someone on whom Christ can rely to speak His words of truth and love?

---

9 Quoting St. Athanasius.

10 Augustine of Hippo, *Sermon* 355.5, in *Sermons 342-400*, trans. Edmund Hill (Hyde Park, NY: New City Press, 1995), 168.

Do you pray for your colleagues at work? What evidence might they have that you belong to Jesus and His Spirit?

What would it mean for you to be more intentional in sharing Christ and His Church with others in ways that would not be off-putting?

What would more study mean for you? Is there a doctrine or Church teaching you need to understand better, and if so, how can you go about doing that?

This is how Saint Paul can urge us all to recognize the empowering we received in our Holy Baptism to become members of Christ's body, living extensions of His own incarnation on earth: "I, then, a prisoner for the Lord, urge you to live in a manner worthy of the call you have received, with all humility and gentleness, with patience, bearing with one another through love, striving to preserve the unity of the spirit through the bond of peace: one body and one Spirit, as you were also called to the one hope of your call; one Lord, one faith, one baptism; one God and Father of all, who is over all and through all and in all" (Eph 4:1–6).

Reread that last line. The beautiful thing about God as Christians know Him is that He does not want to be everything. You and I matter; our neighbors and communities, our experiences and desires all matter. God is not "all," but All in all (Eph 4:6; 1 Cor

15:28). This is what Christianity is all about: a God who empties Himself of being "All" in order to unite lesser beings into Himself in such a way that these mortals are now made immortal. We sinners are made saints; we sons and daughters of Adam and Eve are now adopted children of the heavenly Father.

John Chrysostom, bishop of Constantinople, sought to unite his duties at the altar with those outside the doors of the Church. The "Body of Christ" is revealed as both the Sacred Host as well as one's neighbor, making a powerful union between action and adoration:

> Would you do honor to Christ's body? Neglect him not when naked. Do not honor him here with silken garments, but outside neglect him perishing from cold and nakedness. For the One who said, "This is my body", and by his word confirmed the fact, was also the same One who said, "You saw me hungry, and fed me not; and, inasmuch as you did it not to one of the least of these, you did it not to me (Mt 25:42, 45). Our tasks here in Church require pure hearts, not special garments; what we do outside these doors requires great dedication. Let us learn therefore to be strict in life, and to honor Christ as he himself desires.
>
> For what is the profit, when his table indeed is full of golden cups, but he perishes with hunger? First fill him, being hungry, and then abundantly deck out his table also. Do you behold him in a cup of gold, while you give him not a cup of cold water? And what is the profit? Do you furnish his altar with cloths bespangled with gold, while to himself you cannot afford even the necessary clothing? And what good comes of it? For tell me, should you see one at a loss for necessary food, and omit appeasing his hunger, while you first overlaid his table with silver; would he indeed thank you, and not rather be indignant? What, again, if seeing one wrapped in rags, and stiff with cold, you should neglect giving him a garment, and build golden columns, saying, you were doing it to his honor,

> would he not say that thou were mocking him, and account it a most extreme insult?[11]

> Why do we fast? To commemorate the Passion of the Lamb who, before he was nailed to the cross, underwent insults and brutalities. . . . Isaiah teaches us the rules for a pure and sincere fast: "To loose the bonds of wickedness, to undo the thongs of the yoke, to let the oppressed go free, and to break every yoke . . . to share your bread with the hungry, and bring the homeless poor into your house" (Is 58:6). . . . Do not despise the poor. Ask yourself who they are and you will discover their greatness. They have the face of our Saviour . . . the poor are the stewards of our hope, the guardians of the Kingdom. It is they who open the door to the righteous, and close it to the wicked and self-centred. They are frightening accusers, powerful plaintiffs. . . . Compassion and sharing are things that God loves. They deify the one in whom they dwell . . . they make him the image of the primordial Being, eternal, surpassing all understanding.[12]

Just as all persons were mysteriously "present" in the first Adam, as the New Adam, the Son of God has reunited all persons into His own life. Read the Gospels and see how, even though united with all, Jesus has a special care for the outcast and the frustrated. Those who accept Him as the much-anticipated Messiah receive Him, and He them, with a care and affection not obvious in other encounters. Here God unites not only all peoples by bringing the lowly and the powerful together, He also unites heaven with earth. How we treat one another now is how we shall treat (and be treated by) God forever: "You are all looking forward to greeting Christ seated in heaven. Attend to him lying under the arches, attend to him hungry, attend to him shivering with cold, attend to him needy, attend to him a foreigner. Do it, if it's already your practice; do it, if it isn't your practice. Knowledge of Christian doctrine is

---

11 John Chrysostom, *Homily on Matthew* 50:3-4, New Advent translation, https://www.newadvent.org/fathers/200150.htm, slightly adjusted.

12 Gregory of Nyssa, *On Love of the Poor* §1, in *Roots of Christian Mysticism*, 296.

growing, let good works grow too. You praise the sower; present him with a harvest."[13]

Augustine knew how we must never separate Christian doctrine and good works. "No man has a right to lead such a life of contemplation as to forget in his own ease the service due to his neighbor; nor has any man a right to be so immersed in active life as to neglect the contemplation of God."[14]

As we prepare for the fullness of the Spirit, ask yourself this question: Have I distinguished between my career and my vocation? In your career, you have the necessary work of providing for you and your loved ones, of growing in whatever skillset you have taken on, growing in responsibility, best-practices, and so on. In your vocation, you are called to love and be loved, the necessary work of growing in union with God so you can grow in union with yourself and with all those God has put into your life. "I do not ask that you take them out of the world but that you keep them from the evil one. They do not belong to the world any more than I belong to the world. Consecrate them in the truth. Your word is truth. As you sent me into the world, so I sent them into the world. And I consecrate myself for them, so that they also may be consecrated in truth" (Jn 17:15–19). Your vocation begins by seeing that Jesus has placed you in the world where He needs you—in that career, with these people, in that neighborhood and city. There is no other way to heaven than through these particular and very concrete calls.

Jesus refuses to pray that we leave the world, but He instead ensures to protect us while in this world. He does this by imparting to us His Holy Spirit, our strength and source of the graces to consecrate our daily lives.

> Only when the hour has arrived for his glorification does Jesus promise the coming of the Holy Spirit, since his Death

---

13 Augustine, *Sermon* 25.8, in *Sermons* 20-50, trans. Edmund Hill (Brooklyn: New City Press, 1990), 86.

14 Augustine, *City of God* 19.19, New Advent translation, https://www.newadvent.org/fathers/120119.htm.

> and Resurrection will fulfill the promise made to the fathers. The Spirit of truth, the other Paraclete, will be given by the Father in answer to Jesus' prayer; he will be sent by the Father in Jesus' name; and Jesus will send him from the Father's side, since he comes from the Father. The Holy Spirit will come and we shall know him; he will be with us for ever; he will remain with us. The Spirit will teach us everything, remind us of all that Christ said to us and bear witness to him. The Holy Spirit will lead us into all truth and will glorify Christ. He will prove the world wrong about sin, righteousness, and judgment. (CCC 729)

A fitting image of this Spirit of life is the Seal of God. In Jesus's time, a seal was an authoritative imprint confirming that the contents were authentic and had not been tampered with by the one of the official's enemies. This official mark was embossed upon a missive or official document (or even livestock) to show a direct link between the official who sent it and the person receiving it. This is who the Holy Spirit is for us: Jesus's imprint upon our souls (given to us at our baptism) that God's life dwells within us, that we are His, and that we cannot fall into the hands of the enemy. It was Christ Himself who first declared that He was marked with his Father's seal. For upon this Son of Man, "the Father, God, has set his seal" (Jn 6:27). This is the ultimate goal of Jesus's life in this world, in us—to make not slaves but great lovers whose lives bring us salvation and glorify the Father: "In him we were also chosen, destined in accord with the purpose of the One who accomplishes all things according to the intention of his will, so that we might exist for the praise of his glory, we who first hoped in Christ. In him you also, who have heard the word of truth, the gospel of your salvation, and have believed in him, were sealed with the promised Holy Spirit, which is the first installment of our inheritance toward redemption as God's possession, to the praise of his glory" (Eph 1:11–14).

Imagine that: the Holy Spirit's indwelling within the soul of the baptized is God's "seal," a mark that shows God's promise of making us His own is true. Truth Himself assures us that we would never be alone again, and as His "stamp of approval," God gives us His very Spirit. Or as you might hear assuredly at Mass, "You have found us worthy to be in your presence and minister to you." We have been found worthy to be adopted into the Father's family, and His Holy Spirit is the "first installment" of this new life. "Christ himself declared that he was marked with his Father's seal. Christians are also marked with a seal: 'It is God who establishes us with you in Christ and has commissioned us; he has put his seal on us and given us his Spirit in our hearts as a guarantee.' This seal of the Holy Spirit marks our total belonging to Christ, our enrollment in his service for ever, as well as the promise of divine protection in the great eschatological trial" (CCC 1296).

Your "eschatological trial" is the life right in front of you at this very moment. It is "eschatological" (a theological term referring to the end times and the afterlife) in that everything we do now has an everlasting impact. "And the king will say to them in reply, 'Amen, I say to you, whatever you did for one of these least brothers or sisters of mine, you did for me'" (Mt 25:40). In one sense, we do not have "two lives," as Christians sometimes tend to say. We have only one life, perhaps in two distinct phases: the mere drop in time we spend here on earth and the eternal. But these two moments can never be separated, as we shall spend eternity as an extension of how we choose to live now.

Obviously, then, how we live now matters forever. Every human life has eternal significance. This life is a "trial" because we need to be redeemed and let our "natural" (or what Saint Paul names "fleshy") selves be transformed. This is not easy today, for our society has become so warped that we think that the natural virtues of fidelity and sobriety, of purity and honesty, of justice and courage will win us the Kingdom of God. No. What saves our souls is surrendering to the love of God and letting that love grow in us through interior prayer and outward acts of charity. We are not rewarded for being only human; we must let the Spirit make us *ultra homines*, as Augustine said, more than human! This more will consist of partaking of the Spirit, of drawing our words and thoughts, actions and desires from the divine life to which we have access through the Spirit of God.

Does this image of "seal" mean anything to you? Have you considered the Holy Spirit's indwelling, which you received at Holy Baptism (and strengthened at Confirmation), the means of your joy, your virtue, your purpose?

Take time to reflect on the Lord's promise that He has imprinted His Spirit into your soul and you now enjoy an unbreakable bond between your life and God's.

So we would not relegate things of the Spirit to Sundays and ceremonies, the Spirit who is love also instituted a way of being in "church" that we can often forget: your home. As John Chrysostom preached to the Christians of Constantinople: "For indeed a house is a little Church."[15] Christianity is always trying to get us to see how particular and concrete God has become. This was known by early Christian apologists as the "scandal of the particular" when they had to defend that Christ was *the* Way (not just *a* way), that His Church was *the* Church (not just *a* church), and daresay the same goes for your daily life and *the* "love of your life."

Even though the sacrament of Matrimony begins as a natural reality, Christ's blessing of the chaste love of a man and a woman raises it to the level of a sacrament, which means its very reality imparts grace to those who freely and consciously partake of it. Unlike

---

15 St. John Chrysostom, *Homily* 20 (on Ephesians 5), New Advent translation, https://www.newadvent.org/fathers/230120.htm.

the other six sacraments Christ instituted, the Church teaches that marriage is "endowed with the one blessing not forfeited by original sin nor washed away by the flood."[16] Whereas the sacrament of Baptism was instituted by Christ in the Jordan to wash away original sin, the Mass was given as a continuation of Calvary where our actual sins are washed away by the Lamb's blood, or the Anointing of the Sick where the effects of sin finally catch up to us in a most definitive manner, marriage did not appear because of original sin, and it even remained a constant after the Flood when all else had to be renewed.

The "domestic Church," as we say today, is the home you have built and run, the home in which you have loved and forgiven, cried and laughed. The *Catechism of the Catholic Church* treats the sacrament of Holy Matrimony under the section of a "vocation at the service of communion." Marriage is therefore the vocational way most of the baptized will come to realize not only God's presence but their own eternal identity as well. In the early third century, Tertullian of Carthage reflected on the power of the love between a man and a woman, penning this to his wife:

> What kind of yoke is that of two believers of one hope, one desire, one discipline, one and the same service? Both are brethren, both fellow servants, no difference of spirit or of flesh; nay, they are truly two in one flesh. Where the flesh is one, one is the spirit too. Together they pray, together prostrate themselves, together perform their fasts; mutually teaching, mutually exhorting, mutually sustaining. Equally they are both found in the Church of God; equally at the banquet of God; equally in straits, in persecutions, in refreshments. Neither hides from the other; neither shuns the other; neither is troublesome to the other. The sick is visited, the indigent relieved, with freedom. Alms are given without danger of ensuing torment; sacrifices attended without scruple; daily diligence discharged without impediment. . . . Between the two echo Psalms and hymns; and they mutually challenge each other which shall

16 From the nuptial blessing during the Catholic Mass.

better chant to their Lord. Such things when Christ sees and hears, he joys. To these he sends His own peace. Where two are, present there is also he himself. Where he is, there the evil one is not.[17]

If you are married, do you pray daily that the Holy Spirit increase the love between you and your spouse?

If so, do you and your spouse pray together, celebrate the sacraments together, and carry out the alms together?

Do you see your love for your spouse as holy, as the Holy Spirit binding you together and not just the result of shared histories or initial attraction?

The spouse of the Holy Spirit is traditionally Mary, the one whose "yes" allowed the Son to enter His own creation. She is the perfect disciple, the one saved from the moment of her conception, the spotless daughter of the Father, the mother of the incarnate Son, and the bride of the Holy Spirit. It is more than fitting, then, that the Monday after Pentecost Sunday celebrates the Church's most recent feast, the memorial of the Blessed Virgin Mary, Mother of the Church.

---

17 Tertullian, *To His Wife* 2.8, New Advent translation, https://www.newadvent.org/fathers/0404.htm, slightly adjusted.

In 2018, Pope Francis inaugurated this memorial, placing it into the Roman Calendar on the day immediately following Pentecost. Under the cross, Mary saw her Son give birth to the Church as the waters of Baptism and the Blood of the Holy Eucharist flowed from His lacerated side. As she first experienced with the magi at Epiphany, at Pentecost she saw people flood in from all over the known world to celebrate God's fidelity. The Church is now universal, now on mission. As the Preface for this memorial prays:

> Receiving your Word in her Immaculate Heart,
> She was found worthy to conceive him in her virgin's womb and,
> giving birth to the Creator,
> she nurtured the beginnings of the Church.
> Standing beside the Cross,
> She received the testament of divine love
> and took to herself as sons and daughters
> all those who by the Death of Christ
> are born to heavenly life.
> As the Apostles awaited the Spirit you had promised,
> She joined her supplications to the prayers of the disciples
> and so became the pattern of the Church at prayer.
> Raised to the glory of heaven,
> She accompanies your piligrim Church
> with a Mother's love
> and watches in kindness over the Church's homeward steps,
> Until the Lord's Day shall come in glorious splendor.[18]

18 Mass Preface for Mary, Model and Mother of the Church.

As we conclude this retreat, we invite you to imagine Mary gathered with the earliest Church awaiting the descent of the Holy Spirit.

Imagine her now gazing on people from all over the globe as her own sons and daughters, those very faces for whom her only begotten Son Jesus Christ was freely crucified.

Imagine her now, assumed body and soul into heaven, gazing maternally down upon you as you make your way to the life all the saints will enjoy.

Prayers to the Holy Spirit

Lord, have mercy on us.

Lord, have mercy on us.

Lord, have mercy on us. God the Father of Heaven, have mercy on us.

God the Son, Redeemer of the world, have mercy on us.

God the Holy Spirit, have mercy on us.

Holy Trinity, One God, have mercy on us.

Divine Essence, one true God, have mercy on us.

Spirit of truth and wisdom, have mercy on us.

Spirit of holiness and justice, have mercy on us.

Spirit of understanding and counsel, have mercy on us.

Spirit of love and joy, have mercy on us.

Spirit of peace and patience, have mercy on us.

Spirit of longanimity and meekness, have mercy on us.

Spirit of benignity and goodness, have mercy on us.

Love substantial of the Father and the Son, have mercy on us.

Love and life of saintly souls, have mercy on us.

Fire ever burning, have mercy on us.

Living water to quench the thirst of hearts, have mercy on us.

From all evil, deliver us, O Holy Spirit.

From all impurity of soul and body, deliver us, O Holy Spirit.

From all gluttony and sensuality, deliver us, O Holy Spirit.

From all attachments to the things of the earth, deliver us, O Holy Spirit.

From all hypocrisy and pretense, deliver us, O Holy Spirit.

From all imperfections and deliberate faults, deliver us, O Holy Spirit.

From our own will, deliver us, O Holy Spirit.

From slander, deliver us, O Holy Spirit.

From deceiving our neighbors, deliver us, O Holy Spirit.

From our passions and disorderly appetites, deliver us, O Holy Spirit.

From our inattentiveness to Thy holy inspirations, deliver us, O Holy Spirit.

From despising little things, deliver us, O Holy Spirit.

From debauchery and malice, deliver us, O Holy Spirit.

From love of comfort and luxury, deliver us, O Holy Spirit.

From wishing to seek or desire anything other than Thee, deliver us, O Holy Spirit.

From everything that displeases Thee, deliver us, O Holy Spirit.

Most loving Father, forgive us.

Divine Word, have pity on us.

Holy and divine Spirit, leave us not until we are in possession of the Divine Essence, Heaven of heavens.

Lamb of God, Who takes away the sins of the world, send us the divine Consoler.

Lamb of God, Who takes away the sins of the world, fill us with the gifts of Thy Spirit.

Lamb of God, Who takes away the sins of the world, make the fruits of the Holy Spirit increase within us.

Come, O Holy Spirit, fill the hearts of Thy faithful,
And enkindle in them the fire of Thy love.
Send forth Thy Spirit and they shall be created,
And Thou shalt renew the face of the earth.

Act of Consecration to the Holy Spirit

O Holy Ghost, Divine Spirit of light and love, I consecrate to Thee my understanding, my heart and my will, my whole being, for time and eternity. May my understanding be always submissive to Thy heavenly inspirations and the teachings of the Catholic Church, of which Thou art the Infallible Guide. May my heart be ever inflamed with love of God and of my neighbor. May my will be ever conformed to the Divine will, and may my whole life be a faithful imitation of the life and virtues of our Lord and Savior Jesus Christ, to Whom, with the Father and Thee, be honor and glory forever. Amen.

Daily Consecration to the Holy Ghost

Most Holy Ghost, receive the consecration that I make of my entire being. From this moment on, come into every area of my life and into each of my actions. Thou art my Light, my Guide, my Strength, and the sole desire of my heart. I abandon myself without reserve to Thy Divine action, and I desire to be ever docile to Thine inspirations. O Holy Ghost, transform me, with and through Mary, into another Christ Jesus, for the glory of the Father and the salvation of the world. Amen. (By the Servant of God, Fr. Felix de Jesus Rougier, M.Sp.S.)

Act of Oblation to the Holy Spirit

On my knees before the great cloud of heavenly witnesses, I offer myself body and soul to Thee, eternal Spirit of God. I adore the brightness of Thy purity, the unerring keenness of Thy justice, and the might of Thy love. Thou art the strength and light of my soul. In Thee I live and move and have my being. I desire never to grieve Thee by unfaithfulness to grace, and I pray with all my heart to be kept from the smallest sin against Thee. Make me faithful in every thought, and grant that I may always listen to Thy voice, watch for Thy light, and follow Thy gracious inspirations. I cling to Thee and give myself to Thee, and I ask Thee by Thy compassion to watch over me in my weakness. Holding the pierced feet of Jesus, looking at His five Wounds, trusting in His Precious Blood, and adoring His opened side and stricken Heart, I implore Thee, adorable Spirit, Helper of my infirmity, so to keep me in Thy grace that I may never sin against Thee with the sin which Thou wilt not forgive. Grant to me the grace, O Holy Spirit, Spirit of the Father and of the Son, to say to Thee always and everywhere, "Speak, Lord, for Thy servant hears." Amen. (After a prayer by Cardinal Newman)

May the grace of the Holy Spirit enlighten our hearts and refresh them abundantly with the sweetness of perfect charity!

O Infinite Love, I love Thee; do Thou confirm and increase my love!

O Holy Spirit, sweet Guest of my soul, abide in me and grant that I may ever abide in Thee.

(From the Raccolta)